WHAT DOES IT TAKE TO GET TO

HEAVEN

Sarah,
You have always been
like a sister to me. I
hope you enjoy this book.
I love you,
Tim

WHAT DOES IT TAKE TO GET TO

HEAVEN

TIMOTHY W. BURROW

credo
house publishers

This book is dedicated to my late wife,
Tamara. When I think about how she
lived in love, giving generously to me and
all she encountered, the pain of her loss
cuts a bit deeper. Ironic it seems that,
sometimes, great loss must come before
our eyes are opened to see and journey
upon a path to great gain: Had I not
lost her, I would not have risen as I have
in my hunger to seek heaven, to be with
her, and on that path, to grow in my love
for the Lord and others. Lukewarm in my
ways, I would have remained, and never
seen nor entered the door to the rich new
life that unfolds before those who fully
embrace Christianity. For many reasons,
I love you, my darling Tamara.

Contents

Introduction   ix

1
The Wake-Up Call   1

2
How Many of Us Will Be Saved?   15

3
What Does It Take to Go to Heaven—The Basics   23

4
Need We Simply Believe in Jesus?   29

5
Must We Also Do the Will of God?   33

6
After Being Saved, Can We Lose Our Salvation?   41

7
How Important Is It to Live in Love?   63

8
What Is the Will of God?   79

9
Must We Be Transformed to a New Way of Thinking?   119

10
Are We Automatically Forgiven for Continued Sin?   139

11
It Is Never Too Late to Be Saved   151

12
Final Thoughts   155

Epilogue: A Letter from Heaven   163

Bibliography   167

Scripture Index   169

About the Author   177

Introduction

Congratulations! You decided to embark upon learning how to spend eternity in a place that is much better than this place. In fact, Jesus said that if we knew what it was like, in our joy, we would sell all we have to get it (Matthew 13:44). Yet, few of us have invested much time in learning what it takes to get to heaven.

It's because we're sure we're going there, right? For some of us, we're sure, not based on knowing what God says on the matter, but simply on what we *feel* on the matter, right? And what we feel is based on standards of good and moral conduct, right? But how can we know that our standards match those of God, the sole judge on Judgment Day? For others, we relied on someone telling us what it takes, assuming that person sufficiently studied all that God says on the matter, right? But how do we know that our instructor sufficiently understands all Scripture on the subject? Do we even know if all pastors and priests understand what it takes to go to heaven? I bet your reaction is, "Of course they know—they're pastors and priests." But if they know, why do they disagree on the subject? In fact, well-learned theologians disagree. Whom do we believe?

What *God* says on the matter is in the Bible, and we must turn to the Word ourselves to be *sure* of what it takes to go to heaven. Figuring it out, however, requires a good bit of study, largely because many Scriptures on the subject appear to be inconsistent. For example, we all know that Jesus said that we must believe in Him to be saved, yet the apostle Paul said in 1 Corinthians 15:2 that *"by this gospel you are saved, if you hold firmly to the word I preached to you. Otherwise, you have believed [in Jesus] in vain."* According to this, not only is it not enough to simply believe that Jesus is the Son of God, but following the Bible in a general way is not enough; we are to hold *firmly* to the Word to be saved. As another example, we know that the initial granting of eternal life is easy, for the apostle Paul said that we are saved by grace through faith and not by works, that it is a gift from God (Ephesians 2:8–9). Yet, in response to a question of whether only a few people will be saved, Jesus said to them, *"Make every effort to enter through the narrow door, because many, I tell you, will try to enter and will not be able to"* (Luke 13:24). Why is every effort required if salvation is a gift? Can the gift be lost or taken away? Many more Scriptures appear to be in conflict with others until we study them sufficiently.

Not only are there apparent inconsistencies, there are mysteries. For example, Jesus told us that the gate to eternal life is small, and that only a few find it (Matthew 7:14–15). What is there to find, and what makes the gate small? Jesus also told us that if we are not converted like a child, we will not enter the kingdom of heaven (Matthew 18:3), and unless we are born again, we will not see the kingdom of God (which is heaven) (John 3:3). What does that mean?

My goal is this: I want you to learn for yourself what it takes to go to heaven by reading Scripture on the subject in this book, which is organized in a way to bring clarity to the answer, to show continuity among those that at first appear to be in conflict, and to reveal the true meaning of those that at first seem mysterious or unclear. I began my inquiry on this subject with no plans to write a book and with no agenda, for I simply wanted to know for myself what it takes to go to heaven. I also began by setting aside preconceived notions that could cloud the truth. I decided to incorporate my study into this book upon realizing that many of us have not been accurately taught. Obviously, if we don't learn the truth until Judgment Day, it will be too late.

For you who are not convinced that every word in the Bible is from God, why would you be willing to take a chance by ignoring any of it? Perhaps you have been deceived by recent, trendy declarations of multiple paths to heaven. It can hardly be argued, however, that there is a source of instruction on the matter that is more likely to be accurate than the Bible, and I offer a few reasons: First, nothing in the Bible is inconsistent with historical records. Second, thirty-five miracles of Jesus were told in the collective gospels of Matthew, Mark, Luke, and John, and none have been disproven, though millions of non-believers would seize an opportunity if there were one. It is impossible to explain how the miracles occurred outside of the power of God: Is it possible by some other power or a type of magic to walk on water, to bring life to a man who had been dead for four days, to bring a man to see instantly who had been blind from birth, or to perform any of the other thirty-two miracles?

The high number of miracles and depth and range of the physics-defying power behind them prove that they had to come from God. Jesus has to be who He claimed to be—the Son of God—for God would not perform His miracles through a fraud. Also, God would not have resurrected a dead man who had falsely claimed to be His Son. Therefore, Jesus was not a fraud and His words were true, including His telling us that His words were not His, but God's.

May God's truth on what it takes to go to heaven come to light as you read His Word in this book. Bless all of you, my friends.

~ 1 ~

The Wake-Up Call

On August 9, 2006, I lost Tamara, my wife, my soul mate, the love of my life. With determination, she fought cancer for fourteen months. I just knew that somehow, some way, she would survive.

She didn't.

I entered Tamara's hospital room after having dinner with my son. As I stepped in front of her that evening, with her face directed toward me, she opened her eyes a little and then took her last breath. She had hung on until I arrived—not wanting to die without me. It was 7:22 p.m.

I called her teenage daughters (my stepdaughters), Hannah and Whitney-Lauren, at 7:30 with the news. Just minutes earlier, the heart on Hannah's bracelet had fallen to the ground in the parking lot of the place where they had just finished dinner. The bracelet was actually Tamara's, which Hannah had begun to wear five days earlier when Tamara went into a coma. Whitney-Lauren had said to Hannah, "Quick, pick up the heart, because if you don't, Mom's heart will stop."

At 7:18 p.m., one of Tamara's best friends dropped to her knees next to her truck upon looking at the most beautiful pink sky she had ever seen. Because pink was Tamara's favorite color, she prayed earnestly to God to allow Tamara to die during the time of the pink sky. She knew Tamara's death was imminent. She passed from this life four minutes later. A few hours later that night, the same friend saw a shooting star from her deck. The night before, my son saw a shooting star.

God was communicating to us.

We summoned the family members to Tamara's room at Vanderbilt Hospital in Nashville. While waiting on their arrival, I let down the side rail of Tamara's hospital bed and lay beside her. I wanted to feel the warmth of her body for the last time, before it became cold and firm.

Upon the arrival of the family members, I held closed Tamara's mouth, which had dropped open at the moment of death. I didn't want her girls to feel the coldness from seeing her mouth open, for worse than it being a chilling confirmation that Tamara was completely gone, it depersonalized her. It was still Tamara we were looking at. Through tears and moans, we had our last prayer over her lifeless body.

I was the last to leave the room. I blew kisses at Tamara and into the room as I shut the door, imagining her spirit filling the room as I pulled my eyes away from her body for the last time. It just couldn't be real; it felt like a bad dream. I held a framed picture of her tightly against my chest, clinging to the only thing I had left of her.

"God, I Have to Go to Heaven!"

I went home and gazed at our beautiful house and furnishings. Instantly, it all became meaningless, worthless—mere rubbish. Nothing in this world seemed to matter anymore, other than my family. All that I had worked so hard all my life to achieve, everything I had done to be successful, suddenly meant nothing. As I look back, God, at that moment, began removing the deception of material things.

I walked outside and looked up to a striking full moon, framed by clouds glowing bright white in the moonlight, as beautiful as I had ever seen. Together they cast a warm glow on the earth on a night that was so very cold and dark for me. I kept gazing at the moon and the vast sky, trying to find heaven, trying to find my darling Tamara.

Just before going to bed, I stood in my front yard, connecting with the Lord through prayer and trying to reconnect with my wife. I stared up into the sky. *Where are you, my sweet darling? What are you doing? What are you looking at? What are you thinking? Can you see me now?* Though I was standing in front of my home, I felt completely lost. I was humbled to the core. I looked into the sky and cried, "God, I *have* to go to heaven and be with my sweet darling!" I lifted my arms to the heavens and prayed, "Lord, take me, shape me, mold me, use me. I'll do anything you want."

I believe God planted a new seed in me at that moment. I became ripe for the taking, ripe for further growth in the Lord and Him in me. I surrendered to His will. At that moment, I changed from fixing my eyes on what is seen to what is unseen, for what is seen is temporary, and what is unseen is eternal (2 Corinthians 4:18). It was not about me anymore. It was about following God.

The night of Tamara's death, everything changed. Immediately my thoughts centered on doing whatever it took for God to grant me the blessing of meeting her in heaven someday. We had waited our entire lives to find each other. We were married only two and a half years, and our love and trust, each building on the other, united our hearts in a way that neither of us had ever known. That night, half my heart was ripped from my chest, leaving the other half torn and ragged. Oh, the pain! I kept clinging Tamara's picture to my chest. The hard frame was no substitute for her flesh, for which I so longed. All I had was her spirit, which would forever be with me.

As a sedative for the deep pain that had a firm grip on me, I reached into the hollows of my soul to grasp a ray of comfort in the expectation that someday I would have all of her again, and then never lose her, for we would together be in eternal paradise. Then I reminded myself that I was not even sure of how to get there. After pondering that disturbing thought for just a moment, I said to myself, "This is ridiculous! I've been to church all my life and I don't know what it takes to go to heaven."

It had been a little unsettling throughout my life knowing that I wasn't sure what it took to go to heaven. I was taught repeatedly that I need only believe in Jesus, but I had read Scriptures that certainly suggested that more was required. I kept putting off a quest to reconcile that apparent conflict, justifying my procrastination by telling myself that I was too busy at the moment, that I would do it later, and after all, "I'm a good person and therefore surely I'm going." Little did I know that not only is *being good*—according to the standards of this world— not enough, but also that I have to change the way I think. I also did not realize that God does not automatically forgive a pattern of deliberate sin for the mere asking.

Losing Tamara brought to the forefront of my mind what I knew but ignored, that Judgment Day can fall on anyone at any moment. When I lost her, I felt it absolutely ridiculous that I had been willing to gamble on whether I was on the road to heaven or hell. What can be more important than knowing what it takes to go to heaven?

No More Rolling the Dice

Rolling the dice was over for me. Within days of Tamara's death, I picked up the Bible each day, leaning into every word, in search of anything that would lead me to know what it took to go to heaven, whether direct statements or simply nuggets or clues. I was like a child looking for treasure, but with the critical eye of a lawyer (I am one). I wanted the answer to come from the Word of God, not just from the word of man, which may or may not be a pure reflection of the Word of God. I had not a fleeting thought of writing a book; I simply wanted to know for myself.

> What can be more important than knowing what it takes to go to heaven?

As I began to assimilate Scripture on this subject, my friends were eager to read what I had learned. I asked, "Isn't there a book on this?" My research revealed that very few books were dedicated to answering this question, and all omitted important Scriptures on the subject as well as ignored Scriptures that conflicted with the theory of the author.

So I decided to turn my research into a book. As I compared all Scripture on the subject, I considered various theories of what it takes to go to heaven in search of those that meet with no conflict in Scripture. After well over a thousand hours of study, including multiple readings of the New Testament, reading the works of respected theologians written as far back as 400 years ago, meeting with pastors of various denominations, reading every book I could find on the subject, and comparing hundreds of Scriptures, only one theory stood the test of meeting with no conflict in Scripture on the subject. The results of my study are in this book. All Scripture that addresses, directly and indirectly, what it takes to go to heaven was considered in order to provide assurance that principles espoused were not in conflict with any Scripture on the subject.

Surprising Revelations

I was surprised as to the discovery of some of the basics of what it takes to go to heaven. I became concerned, not just as to my salvation, but also that of Tamara, my family members, and my friends. We

Christians assume that virtually all of us are going to heaven, but Jesus was clear that it requires us to obey God (Matthew 7:21). In fact, we are to repent (Luke 13:5; 2 Peter 3:9), meaning to change not only our thoughts concerning the demands of God for right living, but also our attitude and behavior, and it is to be to such a degree that we are "born again," so to speak (John 3:3). We are to receive the kingdom like a child (Luke 18:17) and change or be converted like a child (Matthew 18:3). Deeds are so important that without them, even our faith is considered dead (James 2:26). Even more surprising to learn was that the kingdom of God can be taken away, not just from the bad apples, but also from those who merely don't produce fruit (Matthew 21:43). Worthless servants can be sent to hell (Matthew 25:14–30). All this will be explained in detail in this book.

Given the above, it is no wonder that few find the small gate (Matthew 7:14). How did I miss these warnings, for I had been to church most of my life? It especially scared me to learn that poor instruction is no excuse for me, for it can shut the kingdom of heaven in my face (Matthew 23:13). *"If a blind man leads a blind man, both will fall into a pit"* (Matthew 15:14).

Anyone who might doubt for a moment that there is no afterlife will have it removed by reading the book *Real Messages from Heaven* by Faye Aldridge (see bibliography). It is a compilation of true stories told by various people who have seen their deceased loved ones reappear in clear images, and in some cases also heard their voice and felt their touch.

The Bible is clear: When we die, only the body dies; our mind and soul live on. Our mind and soul do not live on in another body on earth (reincarnation is a myth). We live on in heaven or hell. There is not a third option. If we go to hell, we will want to die, but we will be there for eternity.

The Bible does not describe what heaven is like. For a description of what it is like, I recommend reading *90 Minutes in Heaven* by Reverend Don Piper (see bibliography), who died for 90 minutes after a car wreck before being prayed back to life. He described heaven as being in another dimension, that even in his happiest moments on earth, he had never felt so fully alive, that he felt more loved than ever before, and that he was removed from all worries, anxieties, and concerns, and felt perfect. I also recommend reading *Within Heaven's Gates* by Rebecca Springer (see bibliography), written in 1898. Like Reverend Piper, Ms. Springer died and came back to life. She described heaven as containing walks made of pearl, bordered on each side by narrow streams of clear water running over stones of gold, that there was no shadow of dust, no taint of decay on fruit or flower, and not a single blade of grass that was not of the brightest green. She recounted that every home had a large garden full of trees and flowers, that the air was soft and balmy, and instead of sunlight, there was a golden and rosy glow everywhere like the afterglow of a Southern sunset in midsummer.

To learn what hell is like, one should read *23 Minutes in Hell* by Bill Wiese (see bibliography). He was granted a 23-minute visit to hell and came back to warn us that it is worse than any of us could imagine. While there, he shared a prison cell with two enormous beasts that paralyzed him with fear. For a time, the light vanished and it became pitch black before one of the beasts threw him against the wall and made him feel as though every bone in his body had been broken. Another beast with razor-like claws and sharp protruding fins attacked him. Flesh hung from his body like ribbons as he fell to the cell floor. He yearned for death, but there would be none. He later escaped the cell and then heard screams of an untold multitude of people crying out in torment. The air was filled with smoke, and a filthy, deathly decaying odor hung in the atmosphere, making it very difficult to breathe. He experienced an insatiable thirst and dryness and desperately longed for just one drop of water. He could see outlines of people through the flames, and the screams from the condemned souls were deafening and relentless. There was no safe place, no safe moment, and no temporary relief of any kind.

I've read every book I can find that describes hell by those who went there during a death experience and came back to share it with others, and some describe a similar level of horror to that described by Mr. Wiese. The Bible gives very little information, other than to describe it as a *"fiery furnace, where there will be weeping and gnashing of teeth"* (Matthew 13:50), a place of *"darkness, where there will be weeping and gnashing of teeth"* (Matthew 25:30), a place of *"eternal punishment"* (Matthew 25:46), *"eternal fire"* (Matthew 25:41), a place of *"torment, and agony in this fire"* (Luke 16:23–24), a place *"where the fire never goes out"* (Mark 9:43), a place of *"wrath and anger"* (Romans 2:8), a *"raging fire"* (Hebrews 10:27), and *"gloomy dungeons"* (2 Peter 2:4).

Hell does not create a second death for us as though we are burned up in the fire and all goes away. Those in hell burn for eternity. The destruction will be *"everlasting"* (2 Thessalonians 1:9), the fire *"eternal"* (Jude 1:7), and the punishment *"eternal"* (Matthew 25:46). Jesus explained in

Luke 16:22–26 that upon one's being sent to hell, nothing can be done to cross over from there to heaven. If we miss our calling, we've missed it forever, and no amount of pleading or repentance will change our immense suffering or allow us to be transferred from hell to heaven. Therefore, we have one chance to get it right, which is here on earth.

Believe in Scripture

At this point in the book, I wish I could go directly into Scripture to prove what it takes to get to heaven. I feel compelled, however, to address some areas that I am finding are being challenged by more and more people. They are the following: whether Scripture is indeed from God; whether entrance into heaven can be only through Jesus; and whether we should listen only to God's Word and not the opinion of man.

The Bible was written by men. How do we know that God told them what to write, and if He did, that they obeyed (as opposed to the words being of their own making)? As stated in Scripture below, the authors of the books of the Bible claimed that what they wrote was from God:

- *"Above all, you must understand that no prophecy of Scripture came about by the prophet's own interpretation. For prophecy never had its origin in the will of man, but men spoke from God as they were carried along by the Holy Spirit"** (2 Peter 1:20–21).
- *"All Scripture is God-breathed and is useful for teaching, rebuking, correcting and training in righteousness, so that the man of God may be thoroughly equipped for every good work"* (2 Timothy 3:16–17).
- *"I want you to know, brothers, that the gospel I preached is not something that man made up. I did not receive it from any man, nor was I taught it; rather, I received it by revelation from Jesus Christ"* (Galatians 1:11; see 1 Corinthians 1:17).

---

* The Holy Spirit (sometimes referred to merely as "Spirit") is God. In Christian theology, the term *trinity* (the actual word *trinity* is not in the Bible) means that there are three eternal distinctions for God—Father, Son, and Holy Spirit. The Bible teaches us that they are separate (references to both "the Son" and "the Spirit of God" throughout the Old Testament, as well as "our image" and "our likeness" in Genesis 1:26), but it also refers to them in the singular as though they are not separate, all three being one divine essence. Think of it both ways as you read Scripture in this book. An analogy is this: Water can be liquid, ice, or vapor; it's the same thing, but in separate forms. The Father, the Son, and the Holy Spirit are the same, but in separate forms.

- *"As for God, his way is perfect; the word of the LORD is flawless"* (2 Samuel 22:31; see Proverbs 30:5).

Not only did the authors of the books referenced above claim that what they wrote was from God, but they also claimed that all other things written or to be written that would eventually make their way into the Bible would be from God. Did God tell them to say that? Obviously, it would be important to God that all Scripture was from Him, and that Scripture itself tells us that. Does He have the power to keep from the Bible any writing that was not of His making? There were great debates over which of the various writings would be included in the Bible. Do we not think that God had the power to control who won each debate?*

Can any of us truly believe that the all-powerful God somehow was unable to control what was included in Scripture, or that some parts slipped by before He realized they were becoming part of the Bible? Do we really believe that on Judgment Day, if we tell God we really tried to live by Scripture, He'll say it was not necessary, that parts of the Bible were incorrect? If that were the case, we would enter heaven questioning God's power because He had allowed the creation of a Bible that was partially a fraud. We would also have to be retrained to know God's will by erasing from our minds that which we learned from the Bible that was not of God. We would enter heaven not confirming what we learned but bewildered and perhaps even rebellious because the Bible misled us. Do we really think God's plan for a perfect heaven would begin that way for us?

Some agree that the Word was appropriate when written, but that it is outdated. The Word declares otherwise: *"The grass withers and the flowers fall, but the word of the Lord stands forever"* (1 Peter 1:25).

Proof of the Validity of Jesus

As to the credibility of the teaching of Jesus, *"while he [Peter] was still speaking, a bright cloud enveloped them, and a voice from the cloud said, 'This is my Son, whom I love; with him I am well pleased. Listen to him!'"* (Matthew

---

* According to the Bible, God can speak into the minds of people (1 Corinthians 12:3, 10–11; 14:24–25), control the minds of people (He hardens whom he wants to harden, Romans 9:18; He hardened the heart of Pharaoh [Exodus 9:12]), and control the minds of animals (Numbers 21:6; 2 Kings 17:25).

17:5). The apostle Mark remembered the event as follows: *"Then a cloud appeared and enveloped them, and a voice came from the cloud: 'This is my Son, whom I love. Listen to him!'"* (9:7). The apostle Luke recounted it as follows: *"While he [Peter] was speaking, a cloud appeared and enveloped them, and they were afraid as they entered the cloud. A voice came from the cloud, saying, 'This is my Son, whom I have chosen; listen to him.' When the voice had spoken, they found that Jesus was alone"* (9:34–36). Matthew, Mark, and Luke wrote their own accounts based on what they respectively claimed to have seen and heard. Either all three lied and no one challenged their lies, the bright cloud and voice was a great magical trick, or it was from God. The only logical choice is the last one, especially when considering that if Matthew, Mark, and Luke conspired to collectively make up the story, their respective accounts of what was said and what occurred would have been without subtle differences as written.

As to the actual teaching of Jesus, were they His or God's? Jesus said they were God's teachings: *"I [Jesus] did not speak of my own accord, but the Father who sent me commanded me what to say and how to say it. I know that his command leads to eternal life"* (John 12:49–50; see John 14:24). Did Jesus lie when He said that? If He lied, then He was not the Son of God, because the Son of God would not lie. But we know that He was the Son of God because of His 35 miracles (this was explained in the Introduction of this book). Therefore, He did not lie, and therefore we know that the words of Jesus (which were reduced to writing by four authors, Matthew, Mark, Luke, and John) are the Word of God.

All know that Jesus taught that entrance into heaven can be only through Him. Most know that John 3:16 is the most quoted Scripture on the subject. It states: *"For God so loved the world that he gave his one and only Son, that whoever believes in him shall not perish but have eternal life."* God gave the modern world ample evidence that John 3:16 is true. In 2012, Tim Tebow was the most celebrated Christian athlete in the United States and perhaps the world. His favorite Scripture was John 3:16, and he proudly displayed "John 3:16" in eyeblack under his eyes during his college games at the University of Florida.

Upon entering the NFL, Mr. Tebow was banned from displaying Scripture under his eyes. God, however, found another way, through Mr. Tebow, to expose John 3:16 not just to those who watched his games, but to many more—90 million people. Mr. Tebow led the Denver Broncos to a victory over the Pittsburgh Steelers in Denver's first playoff game of the season on January 8, 2012. He passed for 316 total yards. His average yards per throw was 31.6, an NFL record. The television rating during the overtime reached 31.6 percent. I was floored when I heard of those three statistics. Later, I learned the following additional statistics. Demaryius Thomas was the receiver who caught the 80-yard pass, the last play of the game that brought the total yards to 316 and the average yards per throw to 31.6. He was born on Christmas Day, and in the same year as Tim Tebow was born. Pittsburgh's time of possession was 31:06 minutes. The game's sole interception was thrown by Pittsburgh when it was third and 16. The January 8, 2012, game was three years to the day after Tim Tebow wore John 3:16 eyeblack on his face at the BCS college championship game. As God's icing on the cake, the last play, an 80-yard touchdown pass, was the first play of overtime, an 11-second overtime victory that was the quickest overtime in NFL history, regular season or post-season.

Anyone who might claim that all these statistics were mere coincidence should ask a statistician. Yes, God had the last say as to banning the Word about His Son. Soon after the game, there were 9,420 tweets per second regarding the game's correlation to John 3:16, Twitter's record at the time for a sporting event, and the second most for any event. That evening and the following day, John 3:16 became the most searched term on Google—more than 90 million times. In conclusion, God gave the world ample evidence on January 8, 2012, that John 3:16 is true, confirming that the only way to enter heaven is through Jesus.

Follow God's Word, Not Man's

On Judgment Day, God will be the sole judge as to whether we go to heaven (James 4:12). Man will not. To learn what it takes to go, should we listen to God or man? Easy answer, huh? Yet, we as a society are moving away from Scripture and turning to the wisdom of man. That makes no sense at all. The apostle Paul warned us of this: *"For the time will come when men will not put up with sound doctrine. Instead, to suit their own desires, they will gather around them a great number of teachers to say what their itching ears want to hear. They will turn their ears away from the truth and turn aside to myths"* (2 Timothy 4:3–4). This is occurring now. People are making up feel-good answers to the question of how to go to heaven.

Some use hollow and deceptive philosophy on the meaning of the Word, which we were also warned about: *"See to it that no one takes you captive through hollow and deceptive philosophy, which depends on human tra-dition and the basic principles of this world rather than on Christ"* (Colossians 2:8). Some add to God's Word, and others take from it, but God told us to do neither: *"Do not add to what I command you and do not subtract from it, but keep the commands of the LORD your God that I give you"* (Deuteronomy 4:2; see Proverbs 30:6). In this book, I will not add to Scripture or subtract from it; otherwise I am presuming to know more of the truth than God knows. Did God do such a good job in creating me that He made me wiser than He is? Proverbs 26:12 says, *"Do you see a man wise in his own eyes? There is more hope for a fool than for him."* As a lawyer, I am trained to present the law to a judge without stretching its meaning or reading something into it that is not there. I used the same approach when presenting Scripture in this book.

Prepare Your Mind to Receive the Depth of the Word

I am hopeful that I sufficiently addressed in previous sections any chal-lenges as to whether the Bible contains God's accurate instructions on how to get to heaven. It is now proper that you prepare your mind to receive the depth of Scripture, to absorb its deeper meaning.

"Do not deceive yourselves. If any one of you thinks he is wise by the stan-dards of this age, he should become a 'fool' so that he may become wise. For the wisdom of this world is foolishness in God's sight" (1 Corinthians 3:18–19). Believe this Scripture. All that we see and read is absorbed in the con-text of our worldly wisdom, which interferes with learning God's wis-dom. God's wisdom is different from the world's wisdom, and if we don't partition off in our minds the world's wisdom, we won't fully grasp God's wisdom in the Word. As to the words *"he should become a 'fool' so that he may become wise,"* we must endeavor to clean our men-tal slate of worldly knowledge when receiving the Word so that God's truth is not tainted or discounted by our preconceived notions, principles, or standards by which we or any-one else lives. To "become a fool," try to blind yourself from the world's view of Scripture and read it from God's view. *"Jesus said, 'For judgment I have come into this world, so that the blind will see and those who see will become blind'"*

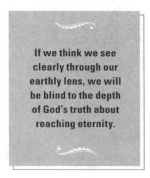

If we think we see clearly through our earthly lens, we will be blind to the depth of God's truth about reaching eternity.

(John 9:39). If we think we see clearly through our earthly lens, we will be blind to the depth of God's truth about reaching eternity.

This applies even to you who already know the Word; read it again as though you are reading it for the first time in this book. Jesus said that life's worries, deceitfulness of wealth, and desires of other things choke the Word, making it unfruitful (Mark 4:19). The ways here take us away from the ways of heaven; that is, the ways here draw us to live in accordance to the ways here and not according to the ways of God. The Word brings us back—if we let it. We let it by reading it as though we are reading it for the first time again, soaking up the depth of the meaning like a sponge. Don't take what is stated in this paragraph lightly. I spent well over one thousand hours over the course of more than seven years writing this book, studying the Word, meditating on it, and comparing and synthesizing Scriptures. Even so, I found that, indeed, life's worries, deceitfulness of wealth, and desires of other things choked the Word, making me less fruitful in some areas than God intends. I had to come back to parts of this book that I had not reviewed for some time in order to realign my way of thinking with God's heavenly way of thinking.

Some verses seem somewhat foolish from a perspective in logic, viewed through a worldly lens. Some verses seem unrealistically demanding, but as your mind is transformed by renewed thinking from absorbing the concepts of Christianity, the demanding Scriptures will no longer seem so demanding. Eventually, you will see that those concepts—heaven's mode of operation—make worldly wisdom seem foolish: *"Has not God made foolish the wisdom of the world? For since in the wisdom of God the world through its wisdom did not know him, God was pleased through the foolishness of what was preached to save those who believe"* (1 Corinthians 1:20–21).

> Going to heaven requires something beyond an event, beyond a decision; it requires a new lifestyle that is counter-cultural, a transformed persona, a rewiring of the way we think, and a reshaping of our hearts.

Do not water down Scripture or discount it by saying, "Surely God does not expect this of us because I don't know anyone else who adheres strictly to this." That merely taints the meaning of Scripture by applying worldly standards. Have full faith in God's Word, for *"He is the Rock, his works are perfect, and all his ways are just"* (Deuteronomy 32:4).

Not only is receiving the depth of the Word the first step on the road to heaven, it brings us to a better life here. I've had a number of friends and associates who are theologically well versed read transcripts of this book as it was being written. Many commented that not only is it sound in explaining what it takes to get to heaven, but it serves as a manuscript on how to carry out one's life as God intends. But the two are inextricable. Going to heaven requires something beyond an event, beyond a decision; it requires a new lifestyle that is counter-cultural, a transformed persona, a rewiring of the way we think, and a reshaping of our hearts. Those changes are evidenced by how we carry out our lives, what we do here on earth, our probationary period wherein we are molded and shaped for the entrance into the true life.

Has this happened to me? Yes, and it feels great.

~ 2 ~

How Many of Us Will Be Saved?

Few of us will be saved. Jesus said, *"Enter through the narrow gate. For wide is the gate and broad is the road that leads to destruction, and many enter through it. But small is the gate and narrow the road that leads to life, and only a few find it"* (Matthew 7:13–14).

Some commentators explain Jesus' statement in this way: Of all the people in the world, only a few hear the message of Jesus, and even if all of them are saved, that is but a few within the context of the world's population. That explanation cannot, however, be reconciled with the statement of Jesus that *"many are invited, but few are chosen"* (Matthew 22:14). It was made at the end of a parable that began by Jesus explaining what the kingdom of heaven is like. Therefore, among those who hear the message of Jesus, not all are chosen—only few are. Notice, too, that Jesus did not say that few accept Him, but that few are chosen, which dispels any notion that all who accept Him—by that alone—are saved.

This frightened me, and I wanted confirmation. Or, to be frank, I didn't want to confirm what frightened me, but I found confirmation in Jesus' response to someone's question of whether only a few people will be saved: He said to them, *"Make every effort to enter through the narrow door, because many, I tell you, will try to enter and will not be able to"* (Luke 13:24). Jesus did not correct the questioner by declaring that more than a few would be saved, and He repeated His statement in

Matthew 7:13–14 that the door to heaven is narrow. Also, He did not say that no effort is required, that some effort is required, or that if we generally do as much as other good people do, that will be enough. He said to make *every* effort.

This is our wakeup call! We are to make *every* effort to enter through the narrow door, because of the many who are invited to accept Jesus, few are chosen. In fact, Jesus said that not only do a few enter the gate, but only a few *find* it. As will be demonstrated in this book, nothing in the Bible contradicts what Jesus said here. Although the Bible is clear that the gate to heaven is opened to everyone who believes in Him, Scripture is clear (as mostly demonstrated in chapters 4, 5, and 6) that it is closed thereafter to those who don't obey. In fact, the apostle Paul said that our belief in Jesus is in vain if we don't hold firmly to the word he preached to us (1 Corinthians 15:2). Moreover, Jesus said in plain words that we can lose what was first given to us: *"Therefore, I tell you that the kingdom of God will be taken away from you and given to a people who will produce its fruit"* (Matthew 21:43). Peter was clear that we are to *do things* to keep our salvation: *"Therefore, my brothers, be all the more eager to make your calling and election sure. For if you do these things, you will never fall, and you will receive a rich welcome into the eternal kingdom of our Lord and Savior Jesus Christ"* (2 Peter 1:10–11; emphasis added). I have read every book I can find on the subject of what it takes to get to heaven, and those that claim that all who believe in Jesus are going no matter how they live their lives ignore many verses of Scripture that tell us otherwise.

> In understanding what it takes to get to heaven, our starting point is this—only a few find the small gate to heaven, and we must make every effort to enter through it—to be reborn to a new way of thinking.

In summary, in understanding what it takes to get to heaven, our starting point is this—only a few find the small gate to heaven, and we must make every effort to enter through it—to be reborn to a new way of thinking. I will provide an abundance of Scripture later in this book to support this truth.

Another very important point is this, and don't let this scare you, for it is the key to receiving joy in living a Christian life. The *fullness* of the joyful life that is available to those who follow Jesus will not come to the halfhearted, but only to those who fully engage. In am not saying that the halfhearted will not receive joy; I am saying that they will not receive the fullness of it. I realize that a full engagement to obey does not seem joyful, but burdensome. It seems antithetical, but the logic of it will come to light as you read this book, especially chapter 9.

Few Understand What It Takes

Does the fact that only a few find the small gate mean that few realize what it takes to go to heaven? I think so. When I began my study, I asked several people what they thought was required. I got varying answers from "just do the right thing as we are faced with situations" to "believe that Jesus is your Savior" to "we're all going to heaven because God is a loving God, and a loving God wouldn't send anyone to hell." But if any of those opinions were accurate, wouldn't the gate be wide, and wouldn't many be chosen? Why don't most of us have the right answer to the question? How much time have we spent trying to find the right answer?

Let's put the matter in perspective based on what we've learned so far:

- We know that on Judgment Day, we are going to heaven or hell,
- We know that heaven is incredibly wonderful, and once we are there, it never ends,
- We know that hell is worse than our worst nightmare, and once we are there, it never ends,
- If we knew what heaven was like, with joy, we would sell all we have to go there, and
- We know that few enter heaven, and therefore most go to hell.

Obviously, nothing can be more important than knowing what it takes to go to heaven, yet many of us will spend less time seeking that answer than we spend planning a vacation. That makes no sense whatsoever. I'm guilty of this insanity myself, for I waited until I was 50 years old before making a diligent inquiry on what it takes to go to heaven.

My study of Scripture began with a search for answers to fundamental questions, erasing from my mind preconceived notions of what I anticipated the answers to be, so as not to interfere with hearing the truth in the Word. *Am I "once saved, always saved," regardless of what I do? Am I bound to unyielding and burdensome rules by which compliance guarantees admittance? Is it something in between?*

I discovered through Scripture, which will be explained in this book, that initial grace of salvation is easy and freely given—I merely need to believe in Jesus Christ. After that, however, I am to repent, which means "to change attitude, thoughts, and behaviors concerning the demands of God for right living,"* and if I turn back, I will not go to heaven. The change is to be so profound that I am to be born again, so to speak, to be converted as a new creation. I cannot do it alone; only with the assistance of the sanctifying work of the Holy Spirit can this be done. I also cannot sufficiently change without having an abundance of love for God and all fellow man. In fact, I am to love the Lord my God with all my heart, soul, mind, and strength, and I am to love my neighbor as myself. If my heart is filled with love for God, I will change my attitude and thoughts concerning the demands of Him for right living, and my behaviors will naturally follow suit.

The paragraph above is the shortest answer given in this book to the question of what it takes to go to heaven. You might want to read it again, for all in this book ties in with it in some fashion.

The title of this book is *What Does It Take to Get to Heaven?* Keeping my salvation is not based on what I do in a vacuum, but on who I become. Although evidence of who I become is from what I do, I am not to focus on doing "what it takes to get to heaven." I focus on being transformed to a new way of thinking, educated by the Word of God, so that love fills me, and my love is manifested by what I do. When I focus on becoming the right kind of person, what I do becomes a natural outflow of me. I will live—from the heart—by the precepts of heaven's mode of operation.

> Seeking heaven is to be done indirectly. We seek to transform our hearts to fully love God and others, in ways as instructed by the Word, and spending eternity in heaven is the by-product of that transformation.

Therefore, seeking heaven is to be done indirectly. We seek to transform our hearts to fully love God and others, in ways as instructed by the Word, and spending eternity in heaven is the by-product of that transformation.

In becoming a new creation, not only will I find heaven in the afterlife, I have been so pleasantly surprised to find that a sprinkling of heaven comes to me here on earth. My life is different: What I felt I lacked in the past is

---

* Goodrick and Kohlenberger, *The Strongest NIV Exhaustive Concordance*, s.v. "repent."

but a memory, replaced by more joy, more peace, and more love. Anxious thoughts rarely come to me. This will be explained at the end of chapter 5.

God Wants All to Be Saved

Seek the truth in earnest, for God wants *all of us* to have eternal life: *"For my Father's will is that everyone who looks to the Son and believes in him shall have eternal life"* (John 6:40).

It is clear that, even as to the worst of us sinners, He wants to cast not one of us away, but for all to be exposed to the true light and to enter the true life! *"The Lord . . . is patient with you, not wanting anyone to perish, but everyone to come to repentance"* (2 Peter 3:9; see Matthew 18:14). God *"accepts men from every nation who fear him and do what is right"* (Acts 10:35). When it comes to salvation, God does not show favoritism (Acts 10:34; Romans 2:11). *"I am not ashamed of the gospel, because it is the power of God for the salvation of everyone who believes"* (Romans 1:16). *"He is the atoning sacrifice for our sins, and not only for ours but also for the sins of the whole world"* (1 John 2:2). Jesus Christ gave himself as a ransom for *all* men (1 Timothy 2:6).

I am so thankful that the Lord is patient with me—with all of us. He wants us to find the narrow gate that leads to eternal life and enter it. We can find the gate only if we hear God through Scripture.

We Must Belong to God Before We Can Hear Him

Only through Scripture can we learn what it takes to go to heaven. This book provides Scriptures that show you what it takes, but we will not fully absorb what God is trying to convey until we decide to belong to Him. Simply listening to God is not enough—we must hear and believe Him. Jesus asked some why His language was not clear to them, why they were unable to hear what He said, and then He explained: *"He who belongs to God hears what God says. The reason you do not hear is that you do not belong to God"* (John 8:47).

If we listen but don't hear, it's because we do not belong to God. Therefore, to go to heaven, we must first decide to belong to God. Then, we can understand His plan for what it takes to go there. Why must we belong to God to hear Him? Why can we not hear God by simply listening? We don't just listen; we absorb, and we will not absorb unless we belong to Him. This is a critical step that cannot be overemphasized. If you are not fully committed to belong to God, I recommend that you put this book down now and pray and meditate and consider committing yourself to Him at this very moment.

To go to heaven, we must first decide to belong to God.

I would not commit, however, until you have decided that turning back is not an option. But don't wait long, for you will never know the time of your last breath. If the thought of committing comes with hesitation, reading this book might help bring you to a state of wanting to commit, which can come suddenly or gradually. An option is to pick a date in the future on which to commit. Upon committing, do not look back and do not fall away. It's a joyful life if you fully engage, and I can assure you that it will come with no regrets.

I did not decide to belong to God until I lost Tamara, and indeed, I developed a deeper understanding of the Word, and it became nourishment for me. I have found that others who suffer loss, endure pain, or suffer financially find it easier to belong to God, seeking His security and protection. In addition to hearing the Word, they grow in faith: *"Listen, my dear brothers: Has not God chosen those who are poor in the eyes of the world to be rich in faith and to inherit the kingdom he promised those who love him?"* (James 2:5).

Those with financial security are less likely to decide to belong to God—many believe they don't need Him so much. This also happened to me, before I lost Tamara. Jesus warned us that it's hard for a rich man to enter heaven (Matthew 19:23), and Paul warned that the love of money is a root of all kinds of evil, stating that some people, eager for money, have wandered from the faith and pierced themselves with many griefs (1 Timothy 6:10). Jesus also warned us that wealth is deceptive (Matthew 13:22). Although being rich makes it harder to go to heaven, it is not impossible: *"Command those who are rich in this present world not to be arrogant nor to put their hope in wealth, which is so uncertain, but to put their hope in God, who richly provides us with everything for our enjoyment. Command them to do good, to be rich in good deeds, and to be generous and willing to share. In this way they will lay up treasure for themselves as a firm foundation for the coming age, so that they may take hold of the life that is truly life"* (1 Timothy 6:17–19).

Overall, money is a dangerous commodity, and if it keeps you from belonging to God, you will not absorb His Word, and without absorbing His Word, you will not follow His Word. It is not worth it, for hell is not worth it—obviously! God warned us: *"What good is it for a man to gain the whole world, yet forfeit his soul?"* (Mark 8:36). Keep everything in perspective, knowing that money is deceptive, wealth might not bring joy, following God does, this life is short, eternity is forever, and we will be forever in hell or in paradise.

Everything we do should be in the context of what it takes to go to heaven. Embrace it! Embrace heaven! Look into the sky. Begin with the end in mind. My eyes are focused more on the afterlife, not so much on this life, which is not even an appetizer of what is to come; ironically, in the process, I experience greater fullness in this life!

~ 3 ~

What Does It Take to Go to Heaven—the Basics

Scripture says it is through grace that we are saved—through faith, not by works—so that no one can boast (Ephesians 2:8–9). Conversely, Scripture also states that faith without deeds is dead (James 2:26), that a person is justified by what he does and not by faith alone (James 3:24), that God will judge each man's work (1 Peter 1:17), and that only he who does the will of God will enter the kingdom of heaven (Matthew 7:21). The following reconciles this apparent conflict, and is the beginning point in knowing what it takes to go to heaven. The moment we decide to believe in Jesus, we receive God's gift of grace, His forgiveness of sins, and eternal life. Our works have nothing to do with it, and grace will not be denied, regardless of the gravity or number of sins we've committed. If we die moments later, we will go to heaven. If, however, we don't repent—meaning to change our attitude and our ways—we will not go to heaven, for our obedience, primarily through deeds, is evidence of our repentance.

Yet even if we embrace a changed life, we will continue to sin. If we confess our sins, we will be forgiven and purified from all unrighteousness, provided that we also forgive others. If we deliberately keep on sinning, we have not repented, at least not sufficiently.

It isn't easy to change our attitude and our ways, nor is it easy to forgive others. We must call for the assistance of the Holy Spirit to walk us through a conversion. It appears that few realize that a conversion is necessary, which I believe is the reason Jesus said that few find the narrow gate. We must find the narrow gate before we can enter it. If the need to convert and the way by which it is achieved were understood by many, then many would, through their conversion, find and enter the gate and travel the road that leads to eternal life.

The numbered points below elaborate on this concept in a more structured way for ease of remembrance. It is a summary of what it takes to go to heaven. It does not reference Scripture, but it references the chapters in this book that provide Scriptural proof of each point:

1. We begin by believing in Jesus. The moment we make that decision, we are cleansed from all sins committed beforehand.* It has nothing to do with our works, for the cleansing is a gift of grace (see chapter 4).
2. We are to repent, which is to change our attitude, thoughts, and behavior toward the demands of God for right living (see Chapters 4 and 5). If not, we will not go to heaven (see chapter 6).†
3. It is the Father's will that we love Him with all our heart, strength, soul, and mind, and our neighbor as ourselves (see chapter 7). We show our love for God by obeying Him, primarily through deeds of service to others, which is His foremost command. (See chapter 8 for God's commands, as spoken through Jesus and the apostles.)
4. Because of our sinful nature, we cannot follow the will of the Father without assistance. We invite the Holy Spirit to live inside us and be our "partner," so to speak. We do this by deciding to belong to God so that we can understand His ways and by surrendering ourselves to Him (see Chapters 3 and 8). That paves the way for Him to live in us, and us in Him, and then with the assistance of the Holy Spirit, through His sanctifying work, we obey (see chapter 9).
5. In time, by sowing to please the Holy Spirit, we become a new

---

*   This assumes that those who claim to believe in Jesus do more than merely declare the words, but are committed by their hearts. This is elaborated on in chapter 6.

†   Chapter 6 provides Scriptural support for the notion that we can lose our salvation. No Scripture states that one's salvation is lost because God quit loving the person. God's love endures forever (Psalm 136, and many other places in the Old Testament). Not having eternal life is caused by our turning away from Him (see chapter 9).

creation, which is our conversion; we are reborn as a selfless person, not selfish as before. As a new creation, our giving and deeds of service to others easily and naturally flow from our heart, and God's commands no longer seem burdensome (see chapter 9). Our changed ways are evidence of our believing in Jesus, not just that He is the Son of God, but that we believe from the heart, consistently with the definition of the original Greek word for "believe" (see chapter 4).

6. The initial granting of our salvation is not earned, nor is keeping it earned, for though we become a new creation, we remain flawed because we will always sin. To be cleansed of sins, we confess them, forgive others and be merciful, do not judge others, not commit the unforgivable sin, and not live according to the sinful nature so that God will continue to forgive us and purify us from all unrighteousness (see chapter 10).

What about the messages that I've heard many Sundays in church that I am forgiven unconditionally for all my sins? I was given the impression that upon accepting Jesus, I'll go to heaven regardless of what I do afterwards, and that so long as I simply ask for forgiveness, all sins will be forgiven, regardless of their degree or frequency. These misconceptions are from making assumptions that have no support in Scripture or by misinterpreting the full message by reading Scriptures in isolation. As a result, the majority of us receive only half the message, that God's salvation is easily attained. We are taught little about what happens if we don't repent. Each Scripture should be read in the context of the New Testament and sometimes in the context of the entire Bible, and especially within the context of the paragraph that it is in, and interpreted accordingly, without making assumptions. Only in that way will we receive the whole message of God.

> The majority of us receive only half the message, that God's salvation is easily attained. We are taught little about what happens if we don't repent.

Stated plainly, our initial grace has nothing to do with our works, but we will not go to heaven, whether it is from falling away from grace or another theory (see chapter 6), if we don't do the will of the Father. We do it as a new creation, and it is by way of a new creation that the small gate to heaven remains open, not by way of earning it, for it is never earned. I urge you to embrace the call to become a new creation, which requires a full engagement. You will be pleased with the "new you," and others will, too.

Any person in any circumstance can become a new creation through the sanctifying work of the Holy Spirit. At a recent visit to a prison in Nashville by a group in our church, I talked to a number of inmates, and most were open and friendly. One stood out as having a peace and joy about him that was immediately recognizable. It was not long after we began talking that I sensed that he had spent a great deal of time in the Word. Upon inquiring as to whether He was close to the Lord, he beamed. Not only did he confirm what I suspected, but he helps other inmates become close to the Lord. No one who *earnestly* seeks God is immune from receiving the sanctifying work of the Holy Spirit and the peace and joy that follow.

The following two pages graphically illustrate the basics of what it takes to get to heaven.

WHAT DOES IT TAKE TO GET TO HEAVEN?

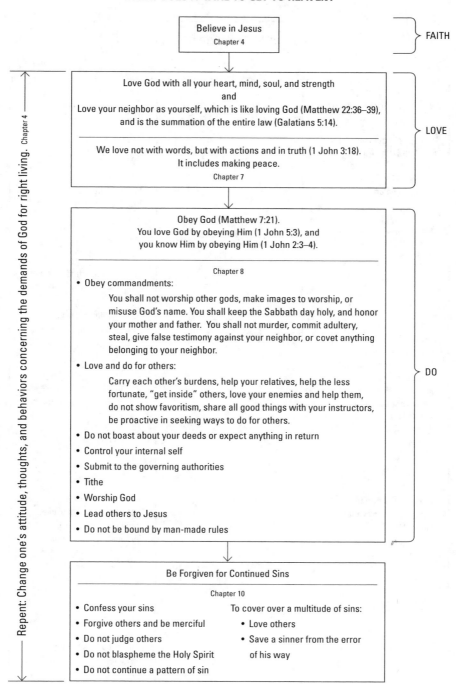

FAITH

Believe in Jesus
Chapter 4

LOVE

Love God with all your heart, mind, soul, and strength
and
Love your neighbor as yourself, which is like loving God (Matthew 22:36–39),
and is the summation of the entire law (Galatians 5:14).

We love not with words, but with actions and in truth (1 John 3:18).
It includes making peace.
Chapter 7

DO

Obey God (Matthew 7:21).
You love God by obeying Him (1 John 5:3), and
you know Him by obeying Him (1 John 2:3–4).

Chapter 8

- Obey commandments:

  You shall not worship other gods, make images to worship, or
  misuse God's name. You shall keep the Sabbath day holy, and honor
  your mother and father. You shall not murder, commit adultery,
  steal, give false testimony against your neighbor, or covet anything
  belonging to your neighbor.

- Love and do for others:

  Carry each other's burdens, help your relatives, help the less
  fortunate, "get inside" others, love your enemies and help them,
  do not show favoritism, share all good things with your instructors,
  be proactive in seeking ways to do for others.

- Do not boast about your deeds or expect anything in return
- Control your internal self
- Submit to the governing authorities
- Tithe
- Worship God
- Lead others to Jesus
- Do not be bound by man-made rules

Be Forgiven for Continued Sins

Chapter 10

- Confess your sins
- Forgive others and be merciful
- Do not judge others
- Do not blaspheme the Holy Spirit
- Do not continue a pattern of sin

To cover over a multitude of sins:
- Love others
- Save a sinner from the error
  of his way

Repent: Change one's attitude, thoughts, and behaviors concerning the demands of God for right living. Chapter 4

"The only thing that counts is faith, expressing itself through love" (Ephesians 5:6).

WHAT DOES IT TAKE TO GET TO HEAVEN?

A RECONDITIONING OF THE MIND

WHAT I DO TO RECONDITION MY MIND	WHAT GOD DOES	THE EFFECT
Change and become like a child (Matthew 18:3).		
Decide to belong to God.		We hear the meaning of the Word (John 8:47).
Obey God, love God, and love others.	God lives in us (John 14:23; 1 John 3:24; 4:12; see Acts 5:32) and the Holy Spirit does His sanctifying work in us (2 Thessalonians 2:13; 1 Peter 1:2).	
Die to old ways of thinking. Rethink everything. Begin at the beginning— like a child, absorb the word of God not to dreadfully learn what we are bound by, but to eagerly learn in what ways we show our love for God and others. Chapter 9.		We are transformed (born again) to a new way of thinking: • Develop a giving nature. • Eager to do what is good. • Scripture becomes nourishment for us. • The "it's about me" way of thinking is removed. • Sinful nature is put off. Chapter 9.
Make every effort to enter through the narrow door (Luke 13:24).		We receive fruits of the Holy Spirit: Love, joy, peace, patience, kindness, goodness, faithfulness, gentleness, and self control (Galatians 5:22–23).
		Yoke is easy; burden is light (Matthew 11:30). Chapter 9.

~ 4 ~

Need We Simply Believe in Jesus?

In the last chapter, we learned the basics of what it takes to get to heaven. We will now address the requirements in more depth.

Most of us have been taught that to go to heaven, we need only to believe in Jesus. To support that belief, preachers and Sunday school teachers often reference Bible verses such as these:

- *"For God so loved the world that he gave his one and only Son, that whoever believes in him shall not perish but have eternal life"* (John 3:16; see John 6:49–51; Acts 16:29–31).
- *"Whoever believes in the Son has eternal life, but whoever rejects the Son will not see life, for God's wrath remains on him"* (John 3:36; see John 8:23–24).

Based on these Scriptures, in order to be saved and go to heaven, we must only "believe" in Jesus. What does "believe" mean? Does it mean that we merely need to believe that Jesus is the Son of God? Need we do anything to help others—even family? Are we not required to go to church, pray, or love and forgive others? Can we steal, commit adultery, even murder, and yet still go to heaven if we believe in Jesus? Can we ignore the needs of others? As long as we believe in Jesus, are we allowed to breach all moral standards in our quest to get ahead financially? If we are required only to believe that Jesus is the Son of God, does that nullify other Scriptures that emphasize the importance of love, obedience, and doing good works? If we believe in Jesus, then can we simply ignore all Scripture that requires us to obey?

"Believe" comes from the Greek word *pisteuō*, which means "to put one's faith in, trust, with an implication that actions based on that trust may follow."* Therefore, "believe" means more than simply believing that Jesus is true or real. Jesus said, *"Why do you call me, 'Lord, Lord,' and do not do what I say?"* (Luke 6:46; see Matthew 7:21). By this statement, Jesus was saying that if we don't do what He says, that means we don't believe in Him.† In addition to that being consistent with the Greek translation for "believe," it is consistent with Hebrews 3:18–19 and 10:36–39,‡ which instruct us that believing and obeying are inextricably intertwined. Therefore, going to heaven requires more than sim-

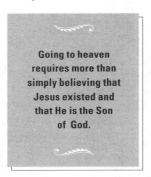

> Going to heaven requires more than simply believing that Jesus existed and that He is the Son of God.

ply believing that Jesus existed and that He is the Son of God. A great number of Christians do not believe that more is required, which amazes me, for that belief requires one to ignore a great deal of Scripture, which will be exposed in this book.

One lady, upon learning that I was writing this book, told me that the answer of what it takes to go to heaven is easy. She stopped and stared at me, and then said "Jesus" and continued to stare as though she bestowed upon me a revelation that I had not considered. I responded, "Jesus, what?" She had little to say that was meaningful. We need to know what the Bible says—all of it—on the subject.

Another person told me that to go to heaven we must trust Jesus. Jesus did not say or even imply that trusting Him was enough. In fact,

---

*   Goodrick and Kohlenberger, *Strongest NIV Exhaustive Concordance*, s.v. "believe."

†   Jesus explained what He meant by this question with a parable illustrating that those who do not put His words into practice will be destroyed because they are not on a good foundation (Luke 6:46–49).

‡   Hebrews 3:18–19 states: *"And to whom did God swear that they would never enter his rest if not to those who disobeyed? So we see that they were not able to enter, because of their unbelief."* Hebrews 10:36–39 states, *"You need to persevere so that when you have done the will of God, you will receive what he has promised. For in just a very little while, 'He who is coming will come and will not delay. But my righteous one will live by faith. And if he shrinks back, I will not be pleased with him.' But we are not of those who shrink back and are destroyed, but of those who believe and are saved."*

no part of the Bible says or implies that. The word "trust" in the Greek definition of "believe" is explained to mean that it is the type of trust that causes actions to follow. Simply trusting that Jesus is truthful or that He will protect us does not get us to heaven.

Believing in Jesus Provides Initial Cleansing

God's grace of eternal life begins with the blood of Jesus washing us from all past sins: Through His blood, we are washed, sanctified, and justified (1 Corinthians 6:9–11; see Acts 13:39; 26:18; Romans 5:9). *"By his wounds [we] have been healed"* (1 Peter 2:24). He was sacrificed as a ransom for us (Mark 10:45). *"God presented him as a sacrifice of atonement, through faith in his blood. He did this to demonstrate his justice, because in his forbearance he had left sins* committed beforehand *unpunished"* (Romans 3:25, emphasis added). See also Romans 4:25.

The blood of Jesus not only washed us of our past sins, it reconciled us to God. *"God was reconciling the world to himself in Christ, not counting men's sins against them"* (2 Corinthians 5:19). *"His purpose was to create in himself one new man out of the two, thus making peace, and in this one body to reconcile both of them to God through the cross, by which he put to death their hostility"* (Ephesians 2:15–16). See Romans 5:10 and Colossians 1:19–20.

In that accepting Jesus as our Savior provides instant cleansing of all sins committed beforehand, and it reconciles us to God, the door to heaven is opened for us. Jesus is our *"author of life"* (Acts 3:15), the true life to come.

If We Repent, We Will Be Forgiven for Our Sins

"All have sinned and fall short of the glory of God" (Romans 3:23), and everyone who sins is a slave to sin (John 8:34). Thus, all of us are slaves to sin. Jesus sets us free from that slavery (John 8:36), and we are instructed to *"stand firm, then, and do not let yourselves be burdened again by a yoke of slavery"* (Galatians 5:1). Putting it together, prior to accepting Jesus, we were slaves to sin, and after accepting Him, we live as free men from that yoke of slavery. We do that by repenting. "Repent" comes from the Greek word *metanoeō*, which means "to change

attitude, thoughts, and behaviors concerning the demands of God for right living."*

Repenting is a part of our being forgiven of our past sins: *"Repent, then, and turn to God, so that your sins may be wiped out, that times of refreshing may come from the Lord, and that he may send the Christ, who has been appointed for you—even Jesus"* (Acts 3:19–20). *"Peter replied, 'Repent and be baptized, every one of you, in the name of Jesus Christ for the forgiveness of your sins'"* (Acts 2:38).

If We Do Not Repent, We Will Perish

If we do not repent, we will not go to heaven: *"Unless you repent, you too will all perish"* (Luke 13:5; see also Matthew 3:2; 4:17). Repentance is such a sure gatekeeper to eternal life that it is referred to as *"repentance unto life"* (Acts 11:18).

The following Scriptures, when taken together, tell us that God wants every one of us not to be stubborn, but to have godly sorrow and repent, for if we don't, we will perish, and He wants that for no one. *"Because of your stubbornness and your unrepentant heart, you are storing up wrath against yourself for the day of God's wrath, when his righteous judgment will be revealed"* (Romans 2:5). *"Godly sorrow brings repentance that leads to salvation and leaves no regret"* (2 Corinthians 7:10; emphasis added). *"The Lord is not slow in keeping his promise, as some understand slowness. He is patient with you, not wanting anyone to perish, but everyone to come to repentance"* (2 Peter 3:9).

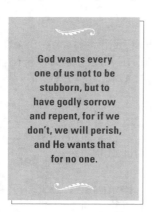

God wants every one of us not to be stubborn, but to have godly sorrow and repent, for if we don't, we will perish, and He wants that for no one.

In conclusion of this chapter, if we believe, as it is defined in the Greek translation, we take action, which is the same as repenting, which means we change our behavior concerning the demands of God for right living. Therefore, merely believing that Jesus is the Son of God is not enough to have everlasting life. The next chapter provides additional confirmation that we are to follow God's will in order to go to heaven.

---

* Goodrick and Kohlenberger, *Strongest NIV Exhaustive Concordance*, s.v. "repent."

~ 5 ~

Must We Also Do the Will of God?

To go to heaven, we learned in the last chapter that we must believe in Jesus and repent. Consistently, the Scriptures below show that we must obey God to go to heaven, which is a part of repenting:

- *"Not everyone who says to me, 'Lord, Lord,' will enter the kingdom of heaven, but only he who does the will of my Father who is in heaven"* (Matthew 7:21).
- *"The world and its desires pass away, but the man who does the will of God lives forever"* (1 John 2:17).
- *"He [Jesus] became the source of eternal salvation for all who obey him"* (Hebrews 5:9).
- *"Now a man came up to Jesus and asked, 'Teacher, what good thing must I do to get eternal life?' . . . 'If you want to enter life, obey the command-ments'"* (Matthew 19:16–17; see Romans 2:6–7).

In addition to obeying God to go to heaven, we must know Him: Jesus prayed, *"Now this is eternal life: that they may know you, the only true God, and Jesus Christ, whom you have sent"* (John 17:3). But this brings us back to obeying God, for as shown below, we come to know Him by obeying His commands:

- *"We know that we have come to know him if we obey his commands. The man who says, 'I know him,' but does not do what he commands is a liar, and the truth is not in him"* (1 John 2:3–4).
- *"They claim to know God, but by their actions they deny him. They are detestable, disobedient and unfit for doing anything good"* (Titus 1:16).

We also must obey Jesus, which is obeying God: Jesus taught, *"I did not come to judge the world, but to save it. There is a judge for the one who rejects me and does not accept my words; that very word which I spoke will condemn him at the last day. For I did not speak of my own accord, but the Father who sent me commanded me what to say and how to say it. I know that his command leads to eternal life"* (John 12:47–50). This Scripture says that on the last day (Judgment Day), God will condemn those who do not accept Jesus and His words, and that His words are God's words. Obeying Jesus is thus the same as obeying God the Father. Because we do not know which day will be our last here, we should begin today to live our lives in a way that we are prepared to have the commands of Jesus repeated to us tomorrow.

We should begin today to live our lives in a way that we are prepared to have the commands of Jesus repeated to us tomorrow.

When considering all Scripture cited so far in this chapter and the last, it is clear that going to heaven requires us to obey God. Think about this for a moment: The Lord's Prayer says in part, *"your will be done on earth as it is in heaven"* (Matthew 6:10), which means that God's will is done in heaven. How can God's will be done in heaven if not all who go there are committed to carrying out His will? As stated previously, Jesus warned us to repent to have eternal life, and He warned us to obey to have eternal life. Consistent with the definition of "repent" as stated in the last chapter, the apostle Paul stated that when we repent and turn to God, we prove our repentance by our deeds (Acts 26:20). In fact, Jesus warned that God will spit out of His mouth those who are lukewarm in deeds: *"I know your deeds, that you are neither cold nor hot. I wish you were either one or the other! So, because you are lukewarm—neither hot nor cold—I am about to spit you out of my mouth. You say, 'I am rich; I have acquired wealth and do not need a thing.' But you do not realize that you are wretched, pitiful, poor, blind and naked"* (Revelation 3:15–17).

I didn't realize that my deeds, or more accurately the lack of them, conveyed to God that I was neither hot nor cold. Worse, I had no idea how much that displeased Him. I thought that when comparing my ways with the ways of the world, I was good enough; I did not realize that I am not to live by the standards of this world (2 Corinthians 10:2), that being "good" according to those standards was not good enough. I also did not know that God, from a time well before Jesus came, punished those who became complacent (Zephaniah 1:12).

I was an "average Joe" in religion and in my relationship with God. In my view, I had been living a godly life: I went to church almost every Sunday; I tithed; I prayed each day for a few minutes, and I read Scripture on the Sundays I chose not to go to church; decisions that affected others I made with their interests in mind; and I took good care of my family.

> I did not realize that I am not to live by the standards of this world (2 Corinthians 10:2), that being "good" according to those standards was not good enough.

I had assumed it was enough. Now I know that it wasn't. I was lukewarm in my walk with the Lord, and the more comfortable my life became, the more lukewarm I became (see Proverbs 30:8–9)—I did not feel the need to earnestly seek to know what God expected of me, and I needed nothing from Him: I had a wonderful wife, son, career, house, car, and no serious issues to deal with. I was taking God for granted. Like the church in Laodicea, I was well fed and not hungry. Looking back, without knowing it, I am virtually certain that I was on the path to destruction.

We Will Not Go to Heaven on Faith Alone

I know a lady who believes that to go to heaven, we must merely have faith that we're going. What? Where did that come from? The Bible clearly says that we are to have faith in Jesus Christ, not just faith that we're going to heaven somehow. No Scripture indicates that simply believing that we're going to heaven increases our chance of getting there. On the contrary, Scripture plainly teaches, *"A person is justified by what he does and not by faith alone"* (James 2:24). Stated more directly, *"faith without deeds is dead"* (James 2:26).

Faith is simply the means by which we live: *"But my righteous one will live by faith"* (Hebrews 10:38), and it is *from* faith that we obey (Romans

1:5). To confirm this, Paul, throughout his epistles, used the word "faith" more than two hundred times, yet none of them is accompanied with the word "alone" or "only." Therefore, faith, by itself, is not enough—it will not save us. We are called to action.

At a party I attended, while overhearing me speak on the subject of what it takes to go to heaven, a gentleman, in somewhat of an aggressive and challenging tone, stated that he does not believe the gate is narrow, as stated by Jesus in Matthew 7:13–14, because from his heart he believes all people go to heaven. He patted his heart as he nodded with conviction as though it were the source of all divine authority. He thought that kind of faith is all it took. Is he kidding? If I believe in my heart that I can fly, should I jump off a balcony and flap my arms? Jude, brother of Jesus and James, warned us that those who *"speak abusively against whatever they do not understand by instinct, like unreasoning animals—these are the very things that destroy them"* (Jude 10). We should not reject the narrow gate analogy based on mere instinct like unreasoning animals. In fact, we shouldn't even rely on the instructions of others, even teachers of the Word, unless they are grounded in truth from Scripture.

Faith, by itself, is not enough—it will not save us. We are called to action.

A Full Engagement

Jesus said that to inherit eternal life we must love the Lord our God with all our heart and with all our soul and with all our strength and with all our mind, and we must love our neighbor as ourselves (Luke 10:25–28). Jesus also said to make every effort to enter through the narrow door (Luke 13:24), and Peter said we are to make every effort to be found spotless, blameless and at peace with Him (2 Peter 3:13–14). God does not want part of me, He wants *all* of me.

Many will resist this. Please don't. As stated before, after Tamara passed, I set aside twenty minutes per day reading the Bible, which increased in time as the Word became more nourishing for me over time. I found that the more I read, the more I understood; the more I understood, the more I wanted more. As I wanted more, I felt more committed to attempt to follow Scripture fully—I wanted all of God;

I wanted to experience all of His beauty and all of His blessings. Upon committing to do my best to live fully in accordance with Scripture, I was surprised that my duty to serve others became a joy, not a burden as it had seemed before. The yoke became light, even though I was doing more. Why is that? At first, I didn't know, other than it being the power of the Holy Spirit.

It was as though a process of conversion came to full fruition in me (chapter 9 explains how that occurs). Although I started the process by deciding to align my life with God, it wasn't I who made the conversion of my deeds becoming a joy; it was God living in me. I began by "stepping out of my own body," so to speak, asking God to live in me and take over. In other words, I began by sowing to please the Spirit by turning my heart to obey the Lord, and the Lord propelled me by giving me the Holy Spirit: God gives the Holy Spirit to those who obey Him (Acts 5:32). Then, the Holy Spirit changed the essence of me by His sanctifying work (2 Thessalonians 2:13; 1 Peter 1:2).

Please do not think that a commitment to obey removes all the fun in life. We are not to grit our teeth and become martyrs, laying our lives on the sacrificial block and denying self at every turn. In fact, upon our nature of giving reaching full maturity, that is, upon being sufficiently transformed by the renewing of our minds (Romans 12:2), giving will be a *means of our pleasure*, and thus not viewed as making great sacrifices. That is the means by which Jesus meets His goal to *"purify for himself a people that are his very own, eager to do what is good"* (Titus 2:14). We became His own, eager to do what is good, and by that eagerness, the yoke is made light and the burden made easy (Matthew 11:30).

To explain, I love riding my bike, taking trips to the beach, attending sports events, seeing movies, and going out to dinner, and I want to have plenty of those moments of entertainment. I know of no Scripture that discourages that whatsoever, so long as we are not wrapped up in self-indulgence (Matthew 23:25; James 5:5). But when our nature of giving reaches maturity, a life that is centered on entertainment will simply not be as rich as a life centered on giving and serving: Although entertaining ourselves will give us bouts of pleasure, which is nice, serving others will penetrate us with joy, joy that lasts. Correspondingly, by our overcoming the passions of the world, the perceived burden of giving will decrease if not be completely removed: *"And his commands are not burdensome, for everyone born of God overcomes the world"* (1 John 5:3–4). This is explained in greater depth in chapter 9.

)vercome the world? That's a tough question, and one with
uld continually examine myself, for worldly ways surround
-in fact, almost hourly—and are continually working to
draw me in, to corrupt me. That's why I pray, "Lord, take me, shape
me, mold me, and use me." So that joy from giving is not robbed from
me, I pray for God to deliver me from evil and the corruption of the
world, which are interferences to developing a giving nature.

A Better Life Here

On losing Tamara, I began to love God like never before, and I longed
to show it by obeying Him. Three months after her death, I committed
to God to do my best to live fully in accordance with Scripture because
it was clear from Scripture itself that obedience was important to Him.
Of course, I will never fully comply because the continual draw from
worldly temptations and my underlying sinful nature will have their
way here and there, but I became seriously committed to do my best.
I wasn't even thinking of benefits that I would receive here. In fact, I
somewhat feared that the sacrifices I would have to make to comply
with Scripture would invite more difficulty and less pleasure to my life.
I overcame those fears by rational thought: "Why would God make my
life less joyful by following Him? Surely, He will reward me for walking out my quest to obey."

That prediction came to be so true. Of the fruit of the Holy Spirit
that is available to us—love, joy, peace, patience, kindness, goodness,
faithfulness, gentleness, and self-control (Galatians 5:22–23)—the
most profound changes in me were in the categories of love, joy, and
peace. I can remember a number of times having my thoughts during
work stop abruptly by a sudden feeling that I had so much love in my
heart that I could not even contain it, and felt as though the excess was
spilling all over the floor.

Also, I was feeling joy even though I had lost the love of my life. I was
amazed that I was even capable of having joy fairly soon after losing her.

As to peace, almost all anxieties left me. The following is an example: After Tamara passed away, I was still trying to make the salon
survive that we opened for her in May 2005, one month before she was
diagnosed with stage 4 cancer. I was losing thousands of dollars every
month. Soon after committing to the Lord to do my best to live fully

in accordance with Scripture, I sent a letter to the landlord asking to be released from the lease, proposing to pay over time the substantial lump-sum payment that was required by the lease if I wanted to cancel it before the end of its term. My proposal offered a corresponding benefit to him in return for the favor I was asking. The salon was draining me financially and I needed to find a way to "stop the bleeding." I had kept the landlord apprised of the situation with my wife, including her passing away, and I was hopeful that his heart would soften somewhat for my situation. I was not optimistic, however, because "business is business."

A few weeks later, my legal assistant handed me a letter from the landlord. I expected a counteroffer or a flat-out rejection, either of which could have a significant impact on my financial health. I distinctly remember that just before reading the letter, a sense of peace came over me, kind of like a shield of peace. My recent commitment to surrender fully to the Lord helped me to trust Him to carry me through all situations for the remainder of my life. I felt comfort in knowing that if the letter were good news, it would be the Lord's blessing, and if it were bad news, I could fight off the arrows of despair by knowing it was the Lord's will (for whatever reason), and that either way, I should rejoice through understanding that God's grace is shown in both ways (2 Corinthians 12:7–10). At a moment when I should have been filled with fear and anxiety, I had none: Apparently, I had received a spirit that removed my slavery to fear (Romans 8:15). I surprised myself. I believe that was the first time in my life that I had that degree of trust in the Lord in that type of situation.

When I read the letter, I dropped to my knees. The landlord was allowing me to discontinue the lease and pay him *nothing*. He waived the substantial sum of money that was required to be paid to end the lease early. In addition to that, he waived back-rent I owed. He had deferred rents in the past in order to help my financial situation because of what my wife and I had been through together, with an understanding that I would repay them at a later date.

I had to read the letter again because it simply could not be true. All seasoned businessmen present a counteroffer that is more favorable to themselves than the original offer. This counteroffer, however, was much better for me and much worse for him than my original offer. The Lord's blessing and grace was beyond anything that I could imagine, which included softening this man's heart and filling it with compassion like I have never seen before in business. I had never even met the man or talked to him; all communications had been through his agent. The Lord's finger of compassion must have touched this man's heart. This was only one of my financial blessings I received right after making my commitment to God to obey.

The more important point of this story, however, is that it illustrates that if we walk in the knowledge that hard times are blessings from the Lord (Romans 5:3–4; Hebrews 12:7–8, 10–11; James 1:2–4), we will be equipped to face hard times with inner peace. Notice that I did not say you *will* face hard times with inner peace; you are simply *equipped* to do so.

As to other areas of the fruit of the Holy Spirit (patience, kindness, goodness, faithfulness, gentleness, and self-control), I still need to improve in some of them and always will, but I can certainly see the difference overall that has come over me. Others have observed the difference as well. By absorbing the Word in earnest and living in a commitment to obey, I was being converted without knowing it, or even knowing that conversion, a born-again state, was the key to finding the narrow gate to heaven.

In addition to this, I received financial blessings. Within two weeks of committing myself to the Lord to do my best to live in accordance with Scripture, from an unsolicited and unexpected phone call, I landed the biggest client I've ever had in my law practice. In each of the subsequent five months, my law practice generated a record in income for the month!

As to today's trendy prosperity preaching, we don't simply claim God's provisions and expect them to come while ignoring God's commands and expectations. The Bible has a different message: We commit to obey, and blessings follow. The blessings will be what we need, or they might be simply what we want. But if what we want is not good for us in the grand scheme of things, God will protect us by giving us only what we need. God, in His infinite wisdom, decides, which is a good thing.

This book is not about improving your life on earth; it's about what it takes to get to heaven. In that quest, however, your life will improve here.

This book is not about improving your life on earth; it's about what it takes to get to heaven. In that quest, however, your life will improve here. I have no doubt about that at all, for it happened to me and I've seen it happen to others.

~ 6 ~

After Being Saved, Can We Lose Our Salvation?

The old order was that salvation followed deeds. The new order is that deeds follow salvation, and if deeds don't follow, we have not repented, and as explained in this chapter, salvation will be lost. (Some believe that those who don't repent were never saved in the first place, a distinction that serves no useful purpose, which is also explained in this chapter.) This should not be confused with the concept of earning our salvation. We never earn our salvation—it is a gift when it is initially granted, and it remains a gift.

> We never earn our salvation—it is a gift when it is initially granted, and it remains a gift.

The "Faith Alone" Scriptures

The "faith alone" Scriptures address the initial granting of salvation, but they do not address whether it is guaranteed no matter how we live our lives afterwards. For example, Ephesians 2:8–9 states, *"For it is by grace you have been saved, through faith—and this not from yourselves, it is the gift of God—not by works, so that no one can boast."* Many hang on this Scripture more than any other for believing that works have nothing to do with salvation. That is true as to the initial granting of salvation.[*] As to the expectation of us after being saved, however, the sentence after Ephesians 2:8–9 (verse 10) states that *"we are God's workmanship, created in Christ Jesus to do good works, which God prepared in advance for us to do."* In other words, after we put our faith in Jesus and are saved, we are created *in Him* to do good works. Neither Scripture addresses what happens if we fail to do good works.

Similar to Ephesians 2:8–9 is Romans 3:28: *"For we maintain that a man is justified by faith apart from observing the law."* Paul stated in the immediately preceding Scriptures (Romans 3:25–26) that, to those who believe in Jesus, God leaves sins committed *beforehand* unpunished. The overall message is that we are granted salvation regardless of the extent to which we observed the law *or* sinned.

What we do afterwards, however, matters. Just after Romans 3:28, Paul confirmed that *after* receiving the grace of salvation, we are to uphold the law: *"Do we, then, nullify the law by this faith? Not at all! Rather, we uphold the law"* (Romans 3:31).[†] Therefore, as in Ephesians 2:8–10, after we put our faith in Jesus and are saved, we are to obey. Also consistent with Ephesians 2:8–9 is Romans 9:30–32: *"What then shall we say? That the Gentiles, who did not pursue righteousness, have obtained it, a righteousness that is by faith; but Israel, who pursued a law of righteousness, has not attained it. Why not? Because they pursued it not by faith but as if it were by works."* The common message of these Scriptures and others (Romans 4:16; 5:1–2; see Luke 7:50; 23:39–43) is that righteousness and salvation are attained through faith alone. None state that we need not do good works afterwards, and as stated above, some declare that we are *expected* to do so. In fact, Paul instructed us that from faith *comes* obedience (Romans 1:5), and by our obedience, we prove our repentance (Acts 26:20). Peter stated that God will judge each man's work (1 Peter 1:17). James confirmed the overall message by stating that one cannot claim to have faith without deeds, and that faith without deeds is dead (James 2:26).

Putting together Scriptures cited so far in this chapter, we do not focus on works as a means to attain salvation; we focus on faith, and

---

[*]   Jesus illustrated by example the ease of being granted salvation. In Luke 23:39–43, the thief on the cross dying next to Jesus made a statement that showed he believed Jesus Christ was the Son of God. Jesus responded by saying that the man would be with Him in paradise. The man was a convicted and admitted criminal, yet was saved by a believing heart and offering but a few words.

[†]   How we are to view the law is touched upon in chapter 8.

from faith, works follow, and if works don't follow, we do not have true faith. This concept is summarized by Paul in Galatians 5:6: *"The only thing that counts is faith expressing itself through love,"* and we express our love with actions and in truth (1 John 3:18).

The "If" Scriptures

What if we claim to have been saved through faith, but don't express our love with actions and in truth? What happens? Many "if" Scriptures tell us that we will not go to heaven. Jesus said that *if* we do not put His words into practice, we will be destroyed because we are not on a good foundation (Luke 6:46–49; see Matthew 7:21; see also 2 Thessalonians 1:8–9). He also said, *"I tell you the truth, if anyone keeps my word, he will never see death"* (John 8:5; emphasis added). Consistently, Paul instructed Timothy that if he watched his life closely, he would save himself (1 Timothy 4:16). Paul also said that *"by this gospel you are saved, if you hold firmly to the word I preached to you. Otherwise, you have believed in vain"* (1 Corinthians 15:2; emphasis added). That Scripture sends a strong message: Our belief in Jesus means nothing if we do not hold *firmly* to the Word.

> We do not focus on works as a means to attain salvation; we focus on faith, and from faith, works follow, and if works don't follow, we do not have true faith.

Peter said, *"Therefore, my brothers, be all the more eager to make your calling and election sure. For if you do these things, you will never fall, and you will receive a rich welcome into the eternal kingdom of our Lord and Savior Jesus Christ"* (2 Peter 1:10–11; emphasis added). Peter said in 2 Peter 3:17 to *"be on your guard so that you may not be carried away by the error of lawless men and fall from your secure position"* (emphasis added).

The writer of Hebrews stated bluntly that we can lose our salvation: "If we deliberately keep on sinning *after we have received the knowledge of the truth, no sacrifice for sins is left, but only a fearful expectation of judgment and of raging fire that will consume the enemies of God. Anyone who rejected the law of Moses died without mercy on the testimony of two or three witnesses. How much more severely do you think a man deserves to be punished who has trampled the Son of God under foot, who has treated as an unholy thing the blood of the covenant that sanctified him, and who has insulted the Spirit of* *grace? For we know him who said, 'It is mine to avenge; I will repay,' and again, 'The Lord will judge his people.' It is a dreadful thing to fall into the hands of the living God"* (Hebrews 10:26–31; emphasis added).* With simple terms, Paul removed any debate on the matter: "If *you live according to the sinful nature, you will die; but* if *by the Spirit you put to death the misdeeds of the body, you will live . . ."* (Romans 8:13; emphasis added).

I am trained as a lawyer to dissect words to expose and consider all views of interpretation. Many hours I have spent reading and studying theories espoused by others on what it takes to go to heaven. It is correct that salvation is never earned, that it is always a gift through the blood of Jesus. But no amount of creativity in interpretation can bring me to conclude that the words "if you live according to the sinful nature, you will die" can mean that you might not. I also cannot dance around other words of Scripture stating plainly that we must obey God to go to heaven (as shown in this chapter, chapter 4, and chapter 5). Those who push aside unappealing Scriptures as though they don't exist, or who convince themselves that someone's opinion can trump contradicting Scripture, will do so to their own peril. Peter warned that ignorant and unstable people distort Scriptures to their own destruction (2 Peter 3:16).

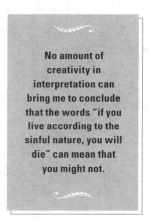

No amount of creativity in interpretation can bring me to conclude that the words "if you live according to the sinful nature, you will die" can mean that you might not.

The Parable of the Unmerciful Servant

Scriptures in this chapter show that not obeying God's commands can cause us to fall from grace of salvation. Forgiving others is one of His commands, and thus, if we do not forgive, we can lose our salvation. The following parable makes that clear:

> Then Peter came to Jesus and asked, "Lord, how many times shall I forgive my brother when he sins against me? Up to seven times?"
> Jesus answered, "I tell you, not seven times, but seventy-seven times.

---

*   This does not mean that all who sin will go to hell. It speaks of living a life of sin. This is explained in chapter 10.

"Therefore, the kingdom of heaven *is like a king who wanted to settle accounts with his servants. As he began the settlement, a man who owed him ten thousand talents was brought to him. Since he was not able to pay, the master ordered that he and his wife and his children and all that he had be sold to repay the debt.*

"The servant fell on his knees before him. 'Be patient with me,' he begged, 'and I will pay back everything.' The servant's master took pity on him, canceled the debt and let him go.

"But when that servant went out, he found one of his fellow servants who owed him a hundred denarii. He grabbed him and began to choke him. 'Pay back what you owe me!' he demanded.

"His fellow servant fell to his knees and begged him, 'Be patient with me, and I will pay you back.'

"But he refused. Instead, he went off and had the man thrown into prison until he could pay the debt. When the other servants saw what had happened, they were greatly distressed and went and told their master everything that had happened.

"Then the master called the servant in. 'You wicked servant,' he said, 'I canceled all that debt of yours because you begged me to. Shouldn't you have had mercy on your fellow servant just as I had on you?' In anger his master turned him over to the jailers to be tortured, until he should pay back all he owed.

"This is how my heavenly Father will treat each of you unless you forgive your brother from your heart" (Matthew 18:21–35; emphasis added).*

This parable at first seemed to have its place in chapter 10, which instructs us on how to receive forgiveness for our sins and the importance of forgiving others. Its instruction, however, is more encompassing than that of forgiveness: It illustrates the operation of the new covenant by showing how to blend Paul's statement in Ephesians 2:8–9—that being saved has nothing to do with our works—with Jesus' instruction that if we do not do the will of God, we will not enter the kingdom of

---

* Jesus begins his parable above by saying "the kingdom of heaven is like . . ." and he ends it with "in anger, his master turned him over to the jailers to be tortured, until he should pay back all he owed." (Matthew 18:34) Does this mean that my torturing will be in heaven, and that it will stop when the punishment is sufficient to cover the degree of my sins? Does it also mean that the debtor, while in heaven, choked a man and put him in prison? Because I can't imagine there being prisons in heaven, reference to the kingdom of heaven must be a metaphor for God's way of analyzing who goes to heaven.

heaven (Matthew 7:21). As we learned in Chapters 3 and 4, the moment we believe in Jesus, we receive God's gift of grace, but if we don't change our ways, we have rejected it. That is the message of Matthew 18:21–35 above, and is the only theory that resolves what might at first appear to be a conflict between Ephesians 2:8–9 and Matthew 7:21. In fact, when considering all Scripture on the subject of what it takes to go to heaven, either directly or indirectly, this is the only theory that conflicts with none of it. The following explains how the parable above illustrates the operation of the new covenant.

In the beginning of this parable, which begins with *"the kingdom of heaven is like,"* the king sentenced the servant to serve his deserved punishment for his debt, which was for him, his wife, his children, and all he had to be sold to repay the debt, which illustrates that, until we are forgiven, we will be held accountable for our sins. But when the man pled for mercy, the master forgave him, even the enormity of his debt (10,000 talents was a great deal of money).* That represented God's initial grace, his initial forgiveness of sins, regardless of its enormity. This is God's *"abundant provision of grace"* (Romans 5:17). It matters not whether our sins are many or few, because, as Paul explains, *"where sin increased, grace increased all the more"* (Romans 5:20).

The debtor offered to pay back everything—by analogy, to do good to the extent required to cover over all his sins. The master, however, took pity on him and canceled the debt and let him go free. Similarly, God wipes our slates clean and does not require us to make amends for our sins. *"In his forbearance he had left sins committed beforehand unpunished"* (Romans 3:25). We are forgiven by grace, not by works. We do not earn our salvation (Ephesians 2:8–9).

What comes next is important: It was the master's will that the servant show his appreciation for the grace given him by having grace toward others, and if he didn't, grace would be removed, and he would be tortured and required to repay all his debt. Likewise, after we receive God's grace, we are to repent (which includes having grace and forgiveness toward others), and if we don't, we will perish (Luke 13:5; 2 Peter 3:9). (This is explained later, in chapter 10.) Therefore, in addition to this parable explaining that we will not be forgiven if we

---

* The first servant owed his master 10,000 talents; 1 talent is approximately 200 pounds of gold. 10,000 talents equals two million pounds of gold. The debt that the fellow-servant owed him was a trifling amount—approximately one five-hundred-thousandth of his own debt. (Barclay, *Matthew*, 2:194)

don't forgive others, and it illustrating that grace has no limits, it also supports Hebrews 10:26–31, which warns that if we deliberately keep on sinning after receiving grace of salvation, there is no sacrifice for sins left.

We can see from this parable that we don't earn our salvation by works, but it can be taken from us if we don't change our ways. The debtor did not earn the release of his debt, but he lost that grace by not changing his ways, and he was punished for the unpaid debt that had earlier been forgiven. His punishment for not forgiving others was not the reinstatement of the original sentence (to be sold to repay the debt); it was worse: He was turned over to the jailers to be tortured until he paid back all he owed. Why? As stated in Hebrews 10:26–31, a man who insults the Spirit of grace under the new covenant has done worse than those who rejected the law of Moses under the old covenant.

We don't earn our salvation by works, but it can be taken from us if we don't change our ways.

Efforts, Producing Fruit, and Working Out Our Salvation

In response to a question of whether only a few people will be saved, Jesus said to make *every effort* to enter through the narrow door, declaring that many will try and not be able to (Luke 13:23–24). Jesus could not have meant that every effort is required only until we decide to believe in Him, otherwise we could get into heaven without believing in Him.* Therefore, even after deciding to believe in Jesus, every effort is required to get to heaven.

Peter also said that we should make every effort: When he said, *"if you do these things, you will never fall, and you will receive a rich welcome into the eternal kingdom"* (2 Peter 1:10–11), he was referring to the following: *"Make every effort to add to your faith goodness; and to goodness, knowledge; and to knowledge, self-control; and to self-control, perseverance; and to perseverance, godliness; and to godliness, brotherly kindness; and to brotherly kindness, love"* (2 Peter 1:5–7).

---

* As explained in chapter 9, it is our every effort, strengthened by the sanctifying power of the Holy Spirit, that transforms us to a newly created person that keeps the small gate to heaven open for us.

Jesus said that our efforts must include producing fruit or the kingdom of God will be taken from us: *"Therefore, I tell you that the kingdom of God* will be taken away from you and given to a people who will produce its fruit"* (Matthew 21:43; emphasis added).

Peter said that we have reason to fear if our efforts are insufficient: *"Since you call on a Father who judges each man's work impartially, live your lives as strangers here in reverent fear"* (1 Peter 1:17; emphasis added). Paul said we have reason to fear if we don't obey: *"Therefore, my dear friends, as you have always obeyed . . . continue to work out your salvation with fear and trembling"* (Philippians 2:12). We need to be diligent to the very end in order to make our hope sure (Hebrews 6:11).

Time Is Limited to Prove Our Repentance by Our Deeds

We know that we are to *"produce fruit in keeping with repentance"* to keep from being *"cut down and thrown into the fire"* (Matthew 3:8-10) and that we are to prove our repentance by our deeds (Acts 26:20). After receiving knowledge of the truth and accepting Jesus as my Savior, will I have a certain amount of time within which to repent before losing my salvation? Before answering that question, let's consider the following parable, which confirms that it is the execution of a promise to live in accordance with God's ways, not the promise itself, that matters.

> *"What do you think? There was a man who had two sons. He went to the first and said, 'Son, go and work today in the vineyard.'*
>
> *"'I will not,' he answered, but later he changed his mind and went.*
>
> *"Then the father went to the other son and said the same thing. He answered, 'I will, sir,' but he did not go.*
>
> *"Which of the two did what his father wanted?"*
>
> *"The first," they answered.*
>
> *Jesus said to them, "I tell you the truth, the tax collectors and prostitutes are entering the kingdom of God ahead of you. For John came to you to show you the way of righteousness, and you did not believe him, but the tax collectors and the prostitutes did. And even after you saw this, you* did not repent and believe him" (Matthew 21:28–32; emphasis added).

---

*   The kingdom of God is heaven (Matthew 19:22–26; Mark 9:47; Luke 13:23–30), as well as the kingdom of God being within us (Luke 11:20–26; 17:20–21). Here, Jesus is referring to heaven.

In the parable above, the second son promised to work in the vineyard but did not go. Jesus used him as an example of those who *"did not repent and believe him"* (Matthew 21:32). Therefore, a mere promise to live in accordance with God's ways is not repenting.

The following parable from Jesus answers the question of whether a *delay* in living a life according to God will cause us to lose our salvation (He said it right after declaring that those who don't repent will perish): *"A man had a fig tree, planted in his vineyard, and he went to look for fruit on it, but did not find any. So he said to the man who took care of the vineyard, 'For three years now I've been coming to look for fruit on this fig tree and haven't found any. Cut it down! Why should it use up the soil?' 'Sir,' the man replied, 'leave it alone for one more year, and I'll dig around it and fertilize it. If it bears fruit next year, fine! If not, then cut it down'"* (Luke 13:6–9). This can mean only that if we do not produce fruit within a sufficient amount of time after receiving our salvation, it will be taken from us. Jesus also warned us in Matthew 21:43 of the danger of not producing fruit: *"Therefore, I tell you that the kingdom of God will be taken away from you and given to a people who will produce its fruit."*

We are to spur each other to produce fruit.

The vineyard caregiver talked the vineyard owner into allowing him to fertilize the tree and give it another year to produce fruit. That means we are to spur each other to produce fruit, to *"spur one another on toward love and good deeds"* (Hebrews 10:24). For more discussion on how we are to help others live a life in Christ, see chapter 8 under the subtopic "Lead Others to Christ."

A Distinction Without a Difference

An abundance of Scripture in this chapter proves that we can fall from grace of salvation. Some people, however, believe, under the "once saved, always saved" theory, that those who are truly saved cannot fall from grace, that the Holy Spirit will not allow them to live according to the sinful nature, and that those who live that way were never saved in the first place. Scripture is clear that one can fall from grace, but it is not clear that every person is saved by merely saying they believe in Jesus without any commitment whatsoever from his or her heart.

Overall, beliefs as to the grace of salvation fall into one of four categories:

1. "Once saved, always saved," and it begins with all who accept Jesus, and salvation is not lost no matter how one lives his or her life afterwards.
2. "Once saved, always saved," but those who live according to their sinful nature after accepting Jesus were never saved in the first place. They don't lose their salvation; they simply never received it for whatever reason. As to those who were saved, however, salvation is not lost no matter how one lives his or her life afterwards.
3. All who accept Jesus are saved, regardless of how committed they are when making the decision, but can lose their salvation if they live according to their sinful nature afterwards.
4. All who accept Jesus are saved, *provided* they are committed when making the decision, but can lose their salvation if they live according to their sinful nature afterwards.

Only one of the above can be the truth. Numbers one and two cannot be true because of the abundance of Scripture that contradicts them. Furthermore, teaching number two has an inconsistency: I know of no preacher who does not promise salvation to *all* who declare their belief in Jesus. It is inconsistent to make that claim, but state later that some were never saved.

Between numbers 3 and 4, Scripture is not clear as to which is correct. It has to be number 4, however, because the Greek definition of "believe," as discussed in chapter 4, connotes a commitment from the heart. For example, what if a person, while drunk when watching a documentary on television about Jesus, says on a whim that he or she indeed believes that Jesus is the Son of God and that He was raised from the dead, and the next day barely remembers saying it, and thinks nothing more about it? Is that person saved? Is that person's belief in accordance with the Greek definition of "believe"? I don't see how that could be. This, obviously, is an extreme example, but it makes the point that there has to be some level of commitment from the heart to be granted salvation. The level that is required is not stated in the Bible, however.

As to which of the beliefs stated above is correct, there is much debate, but let's narrow it down to one issue, which is the only one that really matters: Those who live according to the sinful nature will not go to heaven (Romans 8:13), regardless of the cause. Therefore, it matters not whether one fell from salvation as a result of living according to the sinful nature, or one lived that way because he or she was never saved in the first place. Either way, the result is the same. Therefore, the debate is merely an academic exercise, for *it is a distinction without a difference.*

Why Are We Not Hearing These Warnings in Church?

As to the four beliefs delineated in the last topic, most preachers bring us to believe that number one is the truth. Although I've never heard a preacher expressly say that salvation is guaranteed no matter how one lives his or her life afterwards, the messages of many undoubtedly give that impression. Most convey that when we are saved, we *will* or *should* live like Christians, but I've never heard one address sufficiently the question of what happens if we don't. All say that if we don't, we should ask for forgiveness. But I have not heard a preacher expressly say that that gives us a license to sin as we wish, but the messages of many give that impression. The truth is this: The apostle Paul's warning that if we live according our sinful nature, we will die (Romans 8:13), and Jesus' warning that only he who does the will of the Father will go to heaven (Matthew 7:21), did not come with an escape clause of "but if you ask for forgiveness, sin as you wish." (What we must do or not do to be forgiven for sins committed after being saved is explained in chapter 10.)

Therefore, the majority of us are lulled into complacency and don't even examine ourselves to determine if we are living the Christian life to the level that is conveyed in the Bible. *"Examine yourselves to see whether you are in the faith; test yourselves. Do you not realize that Jesus Christ is in you—unless, of course, you fail the test?"* (2 Corinthians 13:5). Many ignore this Scripture, and some even go so far as to say that the Holy Spirit will *not allow* them to live according to their sinful nature.*

---

* Many who believe that base it on Jesus' statement in John 10:25–30: *"My sheep listen to my voice; I know them, and they follow me. I give them eternal life, and they shall never perish; no one can snatch them out of my hand. My Father, who has given them to me, is greater than all; no one can snatch them out of my Father's hand. I and the Father are one."* We cannot read more into this than what it says: Jesus says that His sheep follow Him and cannot be snatched out of His hand. He did not say that those who declare their belief in Him, whether or not they follow Him afterwards as His sheep, cannot be snatched away. It is simple: If we don't follow Jesus, we are not His sheep, and no Scripture says that we cannot be snatched away.

Why do only a minority of preachers tell us what happens if we do not live a life of obedience? Why do the majority not address Scripture in this chapter that makes it very clear that we can lose our salvation? I used to think that everything spoken from a preacher was with divine authority, and even if not supported by Scripture, they had a deeper understanding that was beyond the plain words. I have come to find that this is not the case. I have listened to a large number of preachers (and small number of priests), and of those who watered down Scripture, made claims not supported by Scripture, or made claims that contradict Scripture, none attempted to provide a basis of authority to justify it, and I have not heard of any such authority. Every time that I heard or read an interpretation of Scripture that does not follow the plain meaning of the words, it is from poor reasoning, from either sloppy thinking or reasoning that is forced to fit a preconceived notion. It is not reasoning from an esoteric meaning understood only by ministers.

For example, the author of a 1,200-page commentary on the New Testament interprets Hebrews 10:26 to apply to only those who were never saved in the first place. The Scripture states that *"if we deliberately keep on sinning after we have received the knowledge of the truth, no sacrifice for sins is left, but only a fearful expectation of judgment and of raging fire that will consume the enemies of God."* The author explains that this applies to a person who knows the way of salvation, he *pretended* to receive it, but then he deliberately repudiates it. What about someone who *indeed* received salvation, but then deliberately sins? The author did not address that situation.

His interpretation narrowed the word "we" to a limited few; to be specific, his interpretation requires words to be added as shown by the following underlined words: *"If we* [not everyone, but only those who were never saved in the first place] *deliberately keep on sinning after we have received the knowledge of the truth, no sacrifice for sins is left, but only a fearful expectation of judgment and of raging fire that will consume the enemies of God."* The author's interpretation means the following: To you who were never saved in the first place, those who deliberately keep on sinning will receive judgment and raging fire, which means that those who do not deliberately keep on sinning will not receive judgment and raging fire, even though they were not saved. But Jesus said without limitation that as to those not saved through Him, God's wrath remains on him (John 3:36). Jesus did not say that as to those not saved through

Him, those who do not deliberately keep on sinning will be saved.

To further show that the author's interpretation is incorrect, it also means the following: To you who were saved in the first place, Hebrews 10:26 means one of two things: either you may deliberately sin, or you are incapable of deliberate sin.

The author's interpretation was obviously forced to fit his preconceived notion, not from an esoteric meaning understood only by ministers. It also reflects sloppy thinking. He would have been better off to throw up his hands and declare that he simply cannot reconcile it with a "once saved, always saved" belief. Remember that this came from a *commentary* on the New Testament, two inches thick, and used by ministers and others for instruction. Incorrect interpretations of Scripture have infiltrated Christians from many sources.

I heard a preacher advise his members that to go to heaven, "all you have to do is repent." *All we have to do is repent?* Wow, that sounds easy. What does that mean, merely saying "I'm sorry," feeling bad for just a moment, a one-time asking for forgiveness, making a confession of faith, or some other easy thing? Repenting to the degree required by God is a complete overhaul of how we think, to become a new creation, to undergo a rebirthing. (This is explained in chapter 9.) If it were easy, Jesus would have not warned us to make every effort to enter through the narrow door, explaining that many will try to enter and not be able to (Luke 13:24).

Most of us don't recognize which instructions from preachers are not supported by or contradict Scripture. For that reason, we need to know the Bible extremely well in order to know the credibility of instructions given to us. Some preachers do their best to stay true to the word and, even so, might slip here or there because, frankly, it takes a great amount of time to deliver a sermon in which everything said is supported by Scripture, and time constraints might come into play. Others might simply choose not to invest the time and deliver messages grounded in sloppy thinking. And still others simply might not be able to overcome their desire to tell people what they want to hear, whether or not their motive is for the purpose of not pushing people away. Churchgoers should be told what they *need* to hear.

As to Christian books written today, many are not true to the Word. For years, I read parts of Christian books at bookstores almost every week. A high percentage of them made a number of claims about how God is or what He will do for us or expects of us that have no support in Scripture whatsoever, and many claims contradicted Scripture.*

This is my plea with preachers, priests, and authors: Please, do not interpret Scripture that requires adding words or taking words away. Please invest sufficient time to make sure that no message or even a point within a message is spoken or written unless there is Scriptural backup, and if there isn't, then qualify it as simply your personal belief that is without Scriptural backup. When you guess as to the desires or ways of God, you might be right and you might be wrong. As to those who convey messages that their book purchasers or tithing church members want to hear, but are contrary to Scripture or that require watering down Scripture, please stop. You are gambling with souls:

- *"If a blind man leads a blind man, both will fall into a pit"* (Matthew 15:14).
- *"Woe to you experts in the law, because you have taken away the key to knowledge. You yourselves have not entered, and you have hindered those who were entering"* (Luke 11:52).
- *"Woe to you, teachers of the law and Pharisees, you hypocrites! You shut the kingdom of heaven in men's faces. You yourselves do not enter, nor will you let those enter who are trying to. Woe to you, teachers of the law and Pharisees, you hypocrites! You travel over land and sea to win a single convert, and when he becomes one, you make him twice as much a son of hell as you are"* (Matthew 23:13–15). (These Scriptures are elaborated on under the topic "Worship the Lord Your God" in chapter 8.)

The above is proof from Scripture that you are gambling with souls. Additional proof is the story below from the book *Nine Days in Heaven* by Dennis and Nolene Prince (see bibliography). It is about Marietta Davis, who, more than 150 years ago, at 25 years old, fell into a trance for nine days and was shown the beauties of heaven and the horrors of hell. Seven months after the vision—at the time and in the manner she had predicted—Marietta died. She wrote a vivid portrayal of her experience that remained in print for 100 years after her death, but the difficult language led to a decline in its popularity, and it was rewritten by

---

* From the Christian books I've read, the best author is C. S. Lewis. He is true to the Word, though in just a very few areas, I believe his views are a bit more strict than the Word. Nevertheless, they are very good to read.

Dennis and Nolene Prince in a manner that was easier to understand, while preserving the accuracy of the original story.

During Ms. Davis' visit to hell, she heard a voice from far above saying, "Marietta, don't be afraid, but study this place of confusion." The voice said later, "Listen! Hear that wild chant! It is coming from the thousands who once sang hymns of worship to the living God without any feeling at all." They were a congregation, and in front of them was their minister wearing priestly robes. At the Gothic pulpit, he tried many times to read from an open book in front of him, but he failed every time. He finally gave up, exhausted, and Ms. Davis realized that his strength was limited and, to a large extent, he was under the control of his audience. The faces of his audience showed deep hatred and maniacal pleasure as they mocked his efforts and delighted at his dreadful agonies. Ms. Davis went on to say:

> While he [the minister] lay there, enveloped in the fires of his own unholy passions, one in his audience stood up and rebuked him. "You fiend of darkness! You child of hypocrisy! Deceiver! Unrivalled deceiver! You are in the hell reserved for the heartless religious teacher! You can never endure enough punishment! You turned religion and the souls of men into nothing more than a means of making a living. Yes, and for this you were even honored and respected! But you took things easy instead of reaching out to the souls of men and women. You did not seek out ruined hearts, and you never brought them the soul-saving truth of heaven. All you did was tell them what they wanted to hear and so you magnified their delusions. Now you are being tormented, and so you should be!"
>
> . . . .
>
> The speaker grated out the words. "Your Maker is just, and you have mocked His majesty. You should have shown the world His glory, and by that light thousands of people should have been led to seek His face."
>
> At this the minister tried to leave, but the speaker continued. "No, you hypocrite! You want to escape but you cannot. Look over this crowd of sufferers and then ask yourself why they are here. Yes, it is true that each of them has sinned and is accountable for their actions. But can you look at them here with a clear conscience, knowing how you have misled them?"

. . . .

As he said these things the whole audience stood up and mocked him in his agony. The spirit who had rebuked him continued to censure him: "You knew very well that we would have done what you told us to do. But when we did wrong things—things that could cause us to end up in this place—you, our supposed teacher of religion, did not try to correct us!

"The Bible, that sacred book, is a gift of God to guide people to heaven! But it was misinterpreted by ministers and theologians like you. You all loved pleasure, your hearts were far from God. Your version of the Bible was a passport to this place!

"Now all we know is bitter grief. Our sins ripen here, and turn into living things. The latest fashions that were once so important to us, bind us now like unquenchable fire. And the money god we all worshiped sits like a ghost in the clouds of death that hang over the abyss.

. . . .

"Do not curse your Maker," he laughed mockingly. "This is your well-earned reward. Listen and I will quote you a Bible scripture that you so often preached so carelessly. Listen to this!

" 'The one who sows to please his sinful nature . . . will reap destruction' (Gal. 6:8). Here is another: 'For the wages of sin is death' (Rom. 6:23).

"Those verses ring so loudly here now. They reach every home of every spirit. They touch every part of our senses. Worse still, they are magnified to the utmost by the doom of this place.

"No, you false teacher, let God and His word be true, for sin has done this to us. We suffered because we have violated God's law."

As he spoke these words he began to tremble violently. He became more and more agitated until he and the rest of the congregation collapsed on the floor. As this happened, they seemed to lose their individualities and began to blend together into a mass of agitated life. Above this mass rose a thick cloud, so dense that it appeared to be a part of the writhing body below.

The sight was too much for me. I could not endure any more of these woeful scenes. I shrank back and cried, "Isn't there a God of mercy somewhere, and can't He see these things and save these people?"

"Yes," declared a voice above me. "Yes, there is a God of mercy. He sees sinners and yearns for them with the greatest compassion. Haven't you read the scripture that says: "For God so loved the world that he gave his one and only Son, that whoever believes in him shall not perish but have eternal life" (John 3:16)?

The voice took on a grieving tone. "But even though salvation is offered to the whole world, even though Christian believers explain it to sinners and plead with them, there are millions who refuse it. Then there are the millions of others who pretend to believe, but have their own false ideas about redemption."

. . . .

The voice continued.

"In the pulpit you saw a false teacher and the bitter consequences of hypocrisy in religion. The people in front of him worshipped in the name of the cross, but without a true reverence for God. They appeared to be worshipping, but their hearts were far away, trying only to please themselves in their devotions. They chose a teacher who wanted only to receive their accolades, so he tried to satisfy their every whim.

. . . .

"Finally Marietta, this scene demonstrated the verse that says, 'If a blind man leads a blind man, both will fall into a pit' (Matt. 15:14). That is what happened here."

The voice paused and continued solemnly, "Marietta, you have had enough of these things, but do not forget them. Never forget that 'the wages of sin is death'" (Rom. 6:23).

Preachers, priests, and Christian authors, your role is extremely important. As we are told by Scripture, and which is confirmed by the story above, your listeners will be held to obey the truth, and your improper teaching will be no excuse for them.

Why Roll the Dice?

Some of you, in spite of the abundance of Scripture to support the proposition that we cannot go to heaven without obeying God, will still not believe it because it is contrary to what you understood for years. Perhaps you are allowing emotions or stubbornness to rule by assuming that the first instructions are always the best ones, or that because you have heard it so many times, it must be true. Would it not be better to challenge what you first learned by asking how one might reconcile those instructions with conflicting Scripture, especially when their plain words leave no room for multiple interpretations?

Another consideration is this: Let's assume for a moment that the "once saved, always saved" belief is correct. How can those who don't believe it be sent into hell for not believing it? For example, on Judgment Day, can anyone imagine God saying the following to those people?: "It is good that you recognized that you were saved by grace, but I have a problem with your also believing that you could fall from grace. I appreciate that after being saved, good works came through your becoming a new creation, especially in the way you helped others, and that you turned away from a pattern of sin. Your salvation, however, was guaranteed. Because you thought it wasn't, I cannot allow you into heaven, and thus, hell is where you will spend eternity." Obviously, God would never hold it against someone for believing one can fall from grace.

Now let's assume for a moment that the "once saved, always saved" belief is *not* correct. What if you believed it, and you did not do the will of God because of that belief, thinking the Holy Spirit carried you along? What if God says to you on Judgment Day, "'*Not everyone who says to [Jesus], "Lord, Lord," will enter the kingdom of heaven, but only he who does [my] will*' [Matthew 7:21]. Did you do my will?" How will you respond? Will you say, "I had to have done your will because after I was saved, the Holy Spirit would not allow me to not do your will." Will God then ignore what you *actually* did or did not do? Will He ignore Peter's warning that He will judge each man's work? (1 Peter 1:17). Will God declare that when Jesus told us to make every effort to enter the narrow door to heaven, that He was actually talking to the Holy Spirit and not us? Will He ignore 2 Corinthians 5:10 (see Revelation 22:12), which says, "*for we must all appear before the judgment seat of Christ, that each one may receive what is due him for the things done while in the body, whether good or bad*"?

What if God also says, "'*I tell you the truth, no one can see the kingdom of God unless he is born again*' [John 3:3]. Have you been born again?" What will you say? Will your "yes" come with credibility if you declare that you took a confession of faith but nothing of substance changed about you?

In conclusion, believing that you can lose salvation and acting accordingly comes with no risk. Believing that salvation is guaranteed, that the gate is wide, that you cannot fall, that the Holy Spirit will not allow you to go against the will of God, and that conflicting Scriptures can be ignored is a dangerous place, for it can lead to complacency and idleness. Paul said that those who are idle should be warned (1 Thessalonians 5:14). Why roll the dice?

Some people will tell you that the conclusions in this chapter are incorrect. Ask them to identify *exactly* which parts they disagree with and to explain why. If they reference Scripture that appears to conflict with Scripture in this chapter, ask them to reconcile them, for God's Word has no mistakes. Check the index of this book to see if it includes the Scripture they claim is conflicting, and read the places in this book where that Scripture is addressed.

How Could a Loving God Send Anyone to Hell?

Our knowledge that God is love (1 John 4:16) can easily seduce us into believing that God surely would not send anyone to hell, but He does. Jesus said: *"I tell you, my friends, do not be afraid of those who kill the body and after that can do no more. But I will show you whom you should fear: Fear him who, after the killing of the body, has power to throw you into hell. Yes, I tell you, fear him"* (Luke 12:4–5; see Matthew 10:28). The parable of the unforgiving servant given earlier in this chapter also proves that God will indeed punish us for not changing our ways after we've been saved. Hebrews 10:26–31 states unequivocally that if we deliberately keep on sinning, we can expect judgment and raging fire. Therefore, though God is loving, He sends people to hell. The Scriptures say what they say, and we should never attempt to discount them to fit our own desires or senses of reasoning.

In my life, I have feared many things: teachers, for they had the power to fail me; my dad, for he had the power to discipline me; my boss, for he had the power to fire me; a girlfriend, for she had the power to break my heart. But I didn't fear the One who has the power to throw me into hell. Honestly, I never really thought about it.

I feared those who, even if they wielded their power, could cause only a temporary setback with no substantive change in my life. But I had not feared the One who can throw me into an eternal fire, from which there is no escape, only eternal pain.

Other places in the Bible warn us that God's wrath is real:*

> For if God did not spare angels when they sinned, but sent them to hell, putting them into gloomy dungeons to be held for judgment; if he did not spare the ancient world when he brought the flood on its ungodly people, but protected Noah, a preacher of righteousness, and seven others; if he condemned the cities of Sodom and Gomorrah by burning them to ashes, and made them an example of what is going to happen to the ungodly; and if he rescued Lot, a righteous man, who was distressed by the filthy lives of lawless men (for the righteous man, living among them day after day, was tormented in his righteous soul by the lawless deeds he saw and heard)—if this is so, then the Lord knows how to rescue godly men from trials and to hold the unrighteous for the day of judgment, while continuing their punishment. This is especially true of those who follow the corrupt desire of the sinful nature and despise authority. (2 Peter 2:4–10)

God's wrath is not just real, it's widespread: It is on all of us until we decide to believe in Jesus: "*Whoever believes in the Son has eternal life, but whoever rejects the Son will not see life, for God's wrath remains on him*" (John 3:36).

Many, if not most, churches avoid speaking of the wrath of God. Their apparent attempt to protect us from the discomfort of fearful messages does us no favors, for it puts us at greater risk of God's wrath in this life—and worse, the everlasting wrath of hell. Jesus pleaded with us over and over again to do what it takes to go to heaven, and He warned us of what sends us to hell (Matthew 5:22; 7:10–28; 11:20–24; 13:24–30, 40–43, 47–50; 18:7–9; 22:1–14; 23:13–36; Mark 8:34–38; 9:42–50; 10:15, 17–27; 11:25; 12:28–34, 38–40; 16:16–18; Luke 6:37–38, 43–49; 9:23–27, 62; 10:16, 25–37; 11:21–28, 39–46; 12:4–10, 13–34, 41–48; 13:1–9, 22–30; 14:12–14; 16:13–15, 19–31; 17:1–10; 18:18–27; 19:11–27; and John 3:3–8). How can anyone assume that God made a mistake when He had Jesus plead to us and warn us as He did? Every word of Scripture is from God, the "*one Lawgiver and Judge,*

---

* "*You who were as numerous as the stars in the sky will be left but few in number, because you did not obey the Lord your God. Just as it pleased the Lord to make you prosper and increase in number, so it will please him to ruin and destroy you*" (Deuteronomy 28:62–63). "*All these curses will come upon you. They will pursue you and overtake you until you are destroyed, because you did not obey the Lord your God and observe the commands and decrees he gave you*" (Deuteronomy 28:45). We should never underestimate the Lord's capacity to become angry. In fact, it can be fierce if we disobey (Exodus 32:12).

the one who is able to save and destroy" (James 4:12). It is simply foolish to ignore any part of His Word.

Awareness of repercussions for not being responsible and obedient motivates us to live as we should, and to the extent we truly *believe* that Jesus was truthful in what he told us, we will obey. The Bible is clear that the fear of the Lord is the beginning of wisdom (Proverbs 9:10; Psalm 111:10) and of knowledge (Proverbs 1:7). It also brings wealth and honor in life (Proverbs 22:4), it puts us in esteem with the Lord (Isaiah 66:2), and it raises his love for us as high as the heavens are above the earth (Psalm 103:11). *"His mercy extends to those who fear him"* (Luke 1:50). The fear of the Lord even moves angels: *"The angel of the LORD encamps around those who fear him, and he delivers them"* (Psalm 34:7). With fear of the Lord being a precept on which many blessings flow, we should not seek to overcome it; conversely, we are to *"always be zealous for the fear of the LORD"* (Proverbs 23:17). It is to delight in (Isaiah 11:3).

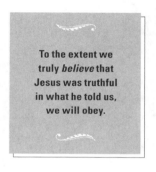

To the extent we truly *believe* that Jesus was truthful in what he told us, we will obey.

I fully realize that being zealous for the fear of the Lord or delighting in fearing Him seems at first to be irrational—why would I delight in fear? Go deeper in what He is saying: Many of God's messages are hints on which to meditate. God wants us to meditate on the Word (Psalm 1:2; 119:23), and doing so brings us to a deeper understanding of His precepts. It is not the fear itself that we should be zealous for and delight in, but it is our being brought to obedience *through fear*. *"The precepts of the LORD are right, giving joy to the heart"* (Psalm 19:8). Have faith in the precepts of the Lord.

~ 7 ~

How Important Is It to Live in Love?

This chapter, chapter 8, and chapter 10 include the main aspects of doing the will of God. In carrying out the Lord's will, we *"do everything in love"* (1 Corinthians 16:14). Love is the foundation of God; it is the foundation of living a Christian life. Let's consider in what ways we are to show our love.

> *On one occasion an expert in the law stood up to test Jesus. "Teacher,"* *he asked, "what must I do to inherit eternal life?"*
>
> *"What is written in the Law?" he replied. "How do you read it?"*
>
> *He answered: "'Love the Lord your God with all your heart and with* *all your soul and with all your strength and with all your mind'; and, 'Love* *your neighbor as yourself.'"*
>
> *"You have answered correctly," Jesus replied. "Do this and you will live."*
>
> *But he wanted to justify himself, so he asked Jesus, "And who is my* *neighbor?"*
>
> *In reply Jesus said: "A man was going down from Jerusalem to Jericho,* *when he fell into the hands of robbers. They stripped him of his clothes, beat* *him and went away, leaving him half dead. A priest happened to be going* *down the same road, and when he saw the man, he passed by on the other* *side. So too, a Levite, when he came to the place and saw him, passed by on* *the other side. But a Samaritan, as he traveled, came where the man was;* *and when he saw him, he took pity on him. He went to him and bandaged*

his wounds, pouring on oil and wine. Then he put the man on his own don-key, took him to an inn and took care of him. The next day he took out two silver coins and gave them to the innkeeper. 'Look after him,' he said, 'and when I return, I will reimburse you for any extra expense you may have.'

"Which of these three do you think was a neighbor to the man who fell into the hands of robbers?"

The expert in the law replied, "The one who had mercy on him."

Jesus told him, "Go and do likewise." (Luke 10:25–37)

With this parable (known as the parable of the good Samaritan), Jesus illustrates that we love our neighbors as ourselves by caring for them. In answering the question of "Who is my neighbor?" Jesus points to a stranger in need. Therefore, "love your neighbor as yourself" means to care for anyone in need, whether we know them or not. This is the second part of the answer to the question in Luke 10:25 of what we must do to inherit eternal life. The first part is to love the Lord your God with all your heart and with all your soul and with all your strength and with all your mind. How do we do that? *"This is love for God: to obey his commands"* (1 John 5:3).[*] As shown by Scripture, the predominant theme of God's commands centers around loving and caring for others. Therefore, loving God means, for the most part, to love and care for others, which is consistent with the parable of the good Samaritan, and which is also consistent with this Scripture:

When they had finished eating, Jesus said to Simon Peter, "Simon son of John, do you truly love me more than these?"

"Yes, Lord," he said, "you know that I love you."

Jesus said, "Feed my lambs."

Again Jesus said, "Simon son of John, do you truly love me?"

He answered, "Yes, Lord, you know that I love you."

Jesus said, "Take care of my sheep."

The third time he said to him, "Simon son of John, do you love me?"

Peter was hurt because Jesus asked him the third time, "Do you love me?" He said, "Lord, you know all things; you know that I love you."

Jesus said, "Feed my sheep." (John 21:15–17)

---

[*] Similarly, loving Jesus also means to obey Jesus' commands (John 14:21) and teaching (John 14:23), which are from God, for Jesus said only what God told Him to say (John 12:49–50).

Jesus' giving more or less the same answer to the same question three times conveys the importance of us showing our love for Him by taking care of others.

Because loving God means to love and care for others, it makes sense that loving my neighbor as myself is considered the summation of the entire law. *"The entire law is summed up in a single command: 'Love your neighbor as yourself'"* (Galatians 5:14). Jesus confirmed the connection between loving God and loving others: *"Hearing that Jesus had silenced the Sadducees, the Pharisees got together. One of them, an expert in the law, tested him with this question: 'Teacher, which is the greatest commandment in the Law?' Jesus replied: '"Love the Lord your God with all your heart and with all your soul and with all your mind." This is the first and greatest commandment. And the second is like it: "Love your neighbor as yourself." All the Law and the Prophets hang on these two commandments'"* (Matthew 22:34–40). Notice Jesus' entree into the second command: "And the second is like it." Therefore, Jesus taught that there is no disconnect between loving the Lord my God with all my heart, soul, and mind, and loving my neighbor as myself. This is put bluntly by the apostle John: *"If anyone says, 'I love God,' yet hates his brother, he is a liar. For anyone who does not love his brother, whom he has seen, cannot love God, whom he has not seen. And he has given us this command: Whoever loves God must also love his brother"* (1 John 4:20–21).

A beautiful example of loving our neighbor is the following fictitious story: Three men were standing in line at the airport on a Friday afternoon, ready to board their plane to return home. They had promised their wives they would be home for dinner on Friday night. While in line, a loud noise drew them to look over to a large display of apples on a table that had been knocked over and were rolling across the floor. The lady selling the apples was blind. One of the men got out of line and approached the blind lady. The other two men said, "Bob, get back in line or you'll miss the plane." Bob replied, "Go ahead, I'll catch the next one." Bob quickly gathered the apples that had rolled across a large part of the floor, people stepping around him, scurrying to be on their way. Bob placed all the apples that were unbruised carefully in one pile and all the bruised apples in another. He counted the bruised apples, and figured the total for the lost apples to be a bit less than $40. He pulled out his wallet, handed $40 to the blind lady, and said, "Here's $40, which should cover the cost of all the damaged apples." As he walked away, the blind lady said, "Sir, excuse me." Bob stopped and turned toward her and said, "Yes." She said, "Are you Jesus?"

Does the Lord expect this level of service from us? It depends, for our instructions are to *"do to others as you would have them do to you"* (Luke 6:31) and to *"love your neighbor as yourself"* (Matthew 22:39). If I were blind and wanted someone to perform that level of service for me, then shouldn't I be willing to perform that level of service for the blind? Do we set our own standards, perhaps, without realizing it?

Jesus taught that when we help others, we are loving God, and when we turn our backs on others, we turn our backs on God. He said, referring to the coming day of judgment:

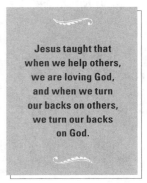

Jesus taught that when we help others, we are loving God, and when we turn our backs on others, we turn our backs on God.

> *Then he will say to those on his left, "Depart from me, you who are cursed, into the eternal fire prepared for the devil and his angels. For I was hungry and you gave me nothing to eat, I was thirsty and you gave me nothing to drink, I was a stranger and you did not invite me in, I needed clothes and you did not clothe me, I was sick and in prison and you did not look after me." They also will answer, "Lord, when did we see you hungry or thirsty or a stranger or needing clothes or sick or in prison, and did not help you?" He will reply, "I tell you the truth, whatever you did not do for one of the least of these, you did not do for me." Then they will go away to eternal punishment, but the righteous to eternal life.* (Matthew 25:41–46; emphasis added)

As much as we may want to ignore the plain meaning of Jesus' words here, it cannot escape us: When we neglect the needs of others, even strangers, we neglect the needs of Jesus, and eternal punishment is our fate. Frederick Dale Bruner is considered by many to be one of the foremost biblical scholars in the nation. In his commentary on Matthew, he states the following regarding this teaching of Jesus:

> What alarms us in hearing this is that no horrible crimes are narrated: it is not murder, adultery, lying, blasphemy, or idolatry that Jesus condemns here, any more than it was heroic virtues that he commended earlier. . . . Nor are other good deeds weighed in a balance. These people may have been faithful in attendance at synagogue, church, mosque, or elsewhere. But it is what they neglected to do, and what is more frightening still, it is what they

neglected to do to that mysteriously "insignificant other" that damns. (Bruner, 927)

If we love God, we must love our brother (1 John 4:21). Because we must love God to go to heaven (Luke 10:27), then we must love our brother to go to heaven. This is confirmed by the following: *"Anyone who hates his brother is a murderer, and you know that no murderer has eternal life in him"* (1 John 3:15).

Jesus came to unite all of us to Him, so that, together, we are one spirit, reconciled to God. *"His purpose was to create in himself one new man out of the two, thus making peace, and in this one body to reconcile both of them to God through the cross, by which he put to death their hostility. He came and preached peace to you who were far away and peace to those who were near. For through him we both have access to the Father* by one Spirit.

"Consequently, you are no longer foreigners and aliens, but fellow citizens with God's people *and members of God's household, built on the foundation of the apostles and prophets, with Christ Jesus himself as the chief cornerstone. In him the whole building is joined together and rises to become a holy temple in the Lord. And in him you too are being built together to become a dwelling in which God lives by his Spirit"* (Ephesians 2:15–22; emphasis added).

In summary, the above states that through the cross, Jesus and all of God's people become one body and one Spirit to reconcile all of us to God. We are fellow citizens in one building in Jesus that rises to become a holy temple in God. *"We are all members of one body"* (Ephesians 4:25). We are members of Christ's body (Ephesians 5:30; 1 Corinthians 12:27), and in Christ, each member belongs to all the others (Romans 12:5), and each part of the body of Christ should have equal concern for each other (1 Corinthians 12:25). In fact, we are to *"submit to one another out of reverence for Christ"* (Ephesians 5:21). God and our fellow man are so reconciled to each other through Jesus that it is inconsistent to praise God and Jesus and yet curse men: *"With the tongue we praise our Lord and Father, and with it we curse men, who have been made in God's likeness. Out of the same mouth come praise and cursing. My brothers, this should not be"* (James 3:9–10).

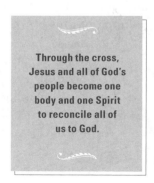

Through the cross, Jesus and all of God's people become one body and one Spirit to reconcile all of us to God.

Also, Jesus and God the Father will live in each of us who love Jesus and obey His teaching. Jesus said, *"If anyone loves me, he will obey my teaching. My Father will love him, and we will come to him and make our home with him"* (John 14:23). Jesus also said, *"I am in my Father, and you are in me, and I am in you"* (John 14:20). *"For in him [God] we live and move and have our being"* (Acts 17:28).

In that God lives in each of us, when we look at others, are we looking at God? When we hurt the feelings of a brother in Christ, are we hurting God, who is living in him? When we walk away from a brother in need, are we walking away from God? Jesus was clear in Matthew 25:45 that whatever we do for the least of our brothers, we do for Him.

I'm picturing myself on Judgment Day, before God in an intimate setting. Although He looks somewhat like a man (it says in Genesis 1:26 that we are created in God's image, but I am speculating as to how distant of an image that might be), the sensation of the depth of Him is indescribable. His eyes are filled with gentleness, kindness, and compassion. I'm reminded of Scripture that speaks of His emotions: jealousy (Exodus 20:5 and 34:14; Deuteronomy 32:21; Nahum 1:20); envy (James 4:5); anger (Deuteronomy 32:16; Ezra 5:12; Psalm 106:32; Zechariah 1:2; Hebrews 3:10–11); love (Psalm 17:7; 25:6; 136; John 17:23); grief (Psalm 78:40; Ephesians 4:30); and sorrow and pain (Genesis 6:6; Jesus' sorrow in Matthew 26:38). Everything I have done, good or bad, is getting ready to be revealed (2 Corinthians 5:10; Revelation 22:12).

God's eyes are fixated on mine, looking past them, into the depth of my soul, and He says, "Do you remember when you were thirty-eight years old and your workmate, Joe, had just been laid off?"

"Yes, Lord," I say.

God continues: "Do you remember him telling you that he was worried, that his wife could not work because they had three children and one of them was autistic and he said he didn't know how he was going to pay his bills?"

"Yes, Lord," I say.

"Did you see that he was on the verge of crying?"

"Yes, Lord," I say.

"Do you remember telling him you were sorry and then walking away, not offering to lift a finger to help him?"

"Yes, Lord," I say.

God's eyes change and you can see the sadness behind them. He leans ever so slightly toward me and says, "You hurt me that day."

My heart sinks. "I am so sorry; how did I hurt you?"

God responds in a soft but piercing tone: "When you looked into Joe's eyes and saw the worry, and said you were sorry and then walked away, in his eyes, you were looking at me. You see, I was living in Joe, and when you looked at him, you looked at me, and what you said to him, you said to me, and when you walked away from him, you walked away from me."

I see two tears running down His cheeks, and I fall to my knees pleading, "Please forgive me, Lord. Please forgive me."

Lord, help me to realize that whatever I don't do for my brothers, I don't do for you.

In summary, all of us who are children of God are one in spirit with Jesus, and together a holy temple in the Lord. Therefore, we are to treat each other as though we are one and the same, that each of us is a different member of the same body, and each of us belongs to the other. This is a concept that is so foreign to our world that it takes true faith to believe it. It brings reasoning to the Word, however, that we are to do unto others as we would have them do unto us.*

The following Scripture sums it up for us. Read it carefully.

> *"As a prisoner for the Lord, then, I urge you to live a life worthy of the calling you have received. Be completely humble and gentle; be patient, bearing with one another in love. Make every effort to keep the unity of the Spirit through the bond of peace. There is one body and one Spirit—just as you were called to one hope when you were called—one Lord, one faith, one baptism; one God and Father of all, who is over all and through all and in all"* (Ephesians 4:1–6; emphasis added).

We Love Not with Words, but with Actions and in Truth

"Dear children, let us not love with words or tongue but with actions and in truth" (1 John 3:18). We love *with* actions and in truth. Actions and truth, without love, gain us nothing:

---

* For further instruction on how we are to treat others, see "Love and Do for Others" in chapter 8.

Now I will show you the most excellent way. If I speak in the tongues of men and of angels, but have not love, I am only a resounding gong or a clanging cymbal. If I have the gift of prophecy and can fathom all mysteries and all knowledge, and if I have a faith that can move mountains, but have not love, I am nothing. If I give all I possess to the poor and surrender my body to the flames, but have not love, I gain nothing. (1 Corinthians 12:31–13:3)

Our loving others is so important to God that it covers over sin. *"Above all, love each other deeply, because love covers over a multitude of sins"* (1 Peter 4:8).

Love Includes Loving Your Spouse

I believe one of the most important responsibilities as a Christian is to live by Christian principles in loving one's spouse. The apostle Peter instructs that wives should be submissive, but that it is even more important that husbands treat their wives with respect and be considerate. He says,

Wives, in the same way be submissive to your husbands so that, if any of them do not believe the word, they may be won over without words by the behavior of their wives, when they see the purity and reverence of your lives. Your beauty should not come from outward adornment, such as braided hair and the wearing of gold jewelry and fine clothes. Instead, it should be that of your inner self, the unfading beauty of a gentle and quiet spirit, which is of great worth in God's sight. For this is the way the holy women of the past who put their hope in God used to make themselves beautiful. They were submissive to their own husbands, like Sarah, who obeyed Abraham and called him her master. You are her daughters if you do what is right and do not give way to fear.

Husbands, in the same way be considerate as you live with your wives, and treat them with respect as the weaker partner and as heirs with you of the gracious gift of life, so that nothing will hinder your prayers. (1 Peter 3:1–7)

Some women are offended by an expectation to be submissive to their husbands. We men should not read more into this Scripture than what it says. It does not state that you need not solicit your wife's opinion on matters involving the two of you, nor does it give you permission to not try to succumb to her wishes. It means no more than this: On matters where you and she differ, you have the authority to make the decision. That privilege can avoid power struggles; it is not to abuse, which would be very unchristian-like.

Adherence to 1 Peter 3:1–7 can bring harmony in a marriage if the husband and wife follow all of it. For us men, it tells us that we are to be considerate and treat our wives with respect. The fact that a husband's prayers will be hindered by his not adhering to this command shows the seriousness of it. If you carry it out to the extent that you put your wife on a pedestal, soliciting her opinion on matters, giving in to her wishes when you are able and it is appropriate, she will probably *want* to submit to you on matters on which you cannot agree, especially if you have the attitude of a true Christian, which is this: *"In humility consider others[, including your wife,] better than yourself"* (Philippians 2:3–4). Overall, the emphasis of 1 Peter 3:1–7 is to love, to truly love, and to have a means to resolve impasses.

To truly love is to have sacrificial love. The apostle Paul emphasized it:

> *Wives, submit to your husbands as to the Lord. For the husband is the head of the wife as Christ is the head of the church, his body, of which he is the Savior. Now as the church submits to Christ, so also wives should submit to their husbands in everything.*
>
> *Husbands, love your wives, just as Christ loved the church and gave himself up for her to make her holy, cleansing her by the washing with water through the word, and to present her to himself as a radiant church, without stain or wrinkle or any other blemish, but holy and blameless. In this same way, husbands ought to love their wives as their own bodies. He who loves his wife loves himself. After all, no one ever hated his own body, but he feeds and cares for it, just as Christ does the church—for we are members of his body. For this reason a man will leave his father and mother and be united to his wife, and the two will become one flesh. This is a profound mystery—but I am talking about Christ and the church. However, each one of you also must love his wife as he loves himself, and the wife must respect her husband.* (Ephesians 5:22–33)

The richness that could come from taking care of a spouse was scarcely known to me until I took care of Tamara after she was diagnosed with cancer. For the first time in my life, I truly put another person's interest ahead of mine. I studied conventional and alternative treatments and talked to a number of health care professionals to determine various ways of treating Tamara's cancer. In addition to two hospital facilities in Nashville, she underwent treatment at Duke University Hospital in Durham, North Carolina; the Block Center in Chicago, Illinois; MD Anderson Clinic in Houston, Texas; CHIPSA hospital in Tijuana, Mexico; and the University of California San Diego hospital.

Every responsibility of mine, professionally and personally, took a back seat to taking care of Tamara. I solicited prayer assistance from her family and friends; I made sure she received the best treatment available; I managed the salon she was supposed to manage (which was opened one month prior to her being diagnosed with cancer). There was nothing for her to do or worry about except to take care of herself.

Tamara and I had been married only eighteen months at the time she was diagnosed. On two occasions during the fourteen months she underwent treatment, she looked at me with her soft brown eyes and asked with gentle humility, "Do you wish you had not married me?" Oh, how I felt sorry for her to ever be confronted with that thought. I assured her that it was a pleasure and an honor to take care of her. It was a lot of work, but I never considered it a burden. She needed me, and I thanked God that He gave her to me and that I had the financial ability and the determination to make sure she had the best care available.

I had been selfish in some ways prior to then, and I actually surprised myself by my devotion to taking care of her. I'm not sure what caused my change in perspective, but I honestly felt that caring for Tamara was an honor. I was glad to serve her. My duty as a husband became a joy, which was part of my blessing from God. For the first time in my life, I learned that joy can follow a full devotion to another person.

The other blessing was that the love and trust between us grew. The more we loved, the more we trusted; the more we trusted, the more we loved. The special bond we shared, embracing each other while waging war against cancer, was a beautiful experience. We were in sync; we had a harmony of hearts. In essence, I was reaping God's reward for carrying the burden of my wife (Galatians 6:2), fulfilling the law of Christ (Colossians 6:1), and providing for my relatives, especially my immediate family (1 Timothy 5:8).

God showered His grace upon me by raising the love between Tamara and me, and it didn't stop there. To make up for the large financial loss of the salon and the loss of income from spending less time in my law practice, God brought me another business deal that made up for those losses. My financial net worth increased during those fourteen months, which amazes me. For the first time, I laid down my life for someone else, not worrying about the financial repercussions of doing so, and God rewarded me for my commitment.

In the end, Tamara died, but Philippians 4:4 says, *"Rejoice in the Lord always. I will say it again: Rejoice!"* I rejoice in all this because *"precious in the sight of the Lord is the death of his saints"* (Psalm 116:15). If it's precious to the Lord, it's precious to Tamara. I can only imagine how wonderful life is for her now in heaven.

As for me, the loss of my wife drew me much closer to the Lord, and I bask in the joy and peace that comes from my relationship with Him. I find myself giving more and more to others, and as I give more, I receive more joy. I would do anything to have my wife back, but I so relish my current relationship with God. More than anything else, however, my changed life gives me the assurance of one day rising to heaven, the true life.

The loss of my wife drew me much closer to the Lord, and I bask in the joy and peace that comes from my relationship with Him.

By her passing, I lost several years on earth with the company of my wife, but I gained by attaining the afterlife by, with the assistance of the Holy Spirit, changing my ways. As a result, I will now have the company of my sweet Tamara for eternity, as well as many others and Jesus Christ.

Love Includes Making Peace

When we are wronged, God commands us to be peacemakers, to turn the other cheek, to forgive unlimited times (see chapter 10), and to not take revenge. Jesus said, *"Blessed are the peacemakers, for they will be called sons of God"* (Matthew 5:9). *"Peacemakers who sow in peace raise a harvest of righteousness"* (James 3:18). *"Make every effort to live in peace with all men and to be holy; without holiness no one will see the Lord. See to it that no one misses the grace of God and that no bitter root grows up to cause trouble and defile many"* (Hebrews 12:14–15).

The apostle Paul tells us that vengeance belongs to God alone: *"Do not repay anyone evil for evil. Be careful to do what is right in the eyes of everybody. If it is possible, as far as it depends on you, live at peace with every-one. Do not take revenge, my friends, but leave room for God's wrath, for it is written: 'It is mine to avenge; I will repay,' says the Lord"* (Romans 12:17–19; see Hebrews 10:30).

Does this mean that we allow others to take advantage of us and mistreat us? I think not, for if a brother sins against you, you are to show him his fault (Matthew 18:15). I believe the overall message is that we are never to engage in a "payback" state of mind, but to leave room for God's wrath and for God to avenge. After all, God has all the information in order to make an accurate assessment of each injustice and the wisdom to know the type and timing of discipline and punishment to impose.

> We are never to engage in a "payback" state of mind, but to leave room for God's wrath and for God to avenge.

Loving others by making peace is so important to God that we are not to even give gifts at the altar without first resolving disputes with our brother. Jesus said, *"Therefore, if you are offering your gift at the altar and there remember that your brother has something against you, leave your gift there in front of the altar. First go and be reconciled to your brother; then come and offer your gift. Settle matters quickly with your adversary who is taking you to court. Do it while you are still with him on the way, or he may hand you over to the judge, and the judge may hand you over to the officer, and you may be thrown into prison. I tell you the truth, you will not get out until you have paid the last penny"* (Matthew 5:23–26).

We learned through Scripture that because of our sins, God sent His Son to reconcile us to Him through Christ, not counting our sins against us (2 Corinthians 5:17–19; Ephesians 2:16; Colossians 1:19–20). God expects the same of us, that we be reconciled to our brothers. We should begin by covering over an offense (act as though it did not happen), which promotes love (Proverbs 17:9) and is to our glory (Proverbs 19:11). And we should never stir up dissension among brothers, which God detests (Proverbs 6:19). In fact, we are to warn a divisive person once, and then warn him a second time, and after that, have nothing to do with him (Titus 3:10).

In keeping peace, we are to guard what we say: *"If anyone considers himself religious and yet does not keep a tight rein on his tongue, he deceives himself and his religion is worthless"* (James 1:26). We're not even to be angry at others or call them names: Jesus said, *"I tell you that anyone who is angry with his brother will be subject to judgment. Again, anyone who says to his brother, 'Raca' is answerable to the Sanhedrin. But anyone who says, 'You fool!' will be in danger of the fire of hell"* (Matthew 5:22). This one surprised me at first. When angry or frustrated, especially at other drivers, I used to call people adjective-spiced names under my breath. I never thought for a moment that it would put me in danger of the fire of hell. How can this be if no one hears me and therefore I'm not hurting anyone? Perhaps Jesus is telling us that the problem is not our coarse words, but the heart from which our words flow. We are to love everyone and forgive all offensive acts, even the minor ones.

From all this, it is obvious that God expects our love to rise to a level that is much higher than that which we observe of most people here on earth. It is as though we are to become here like those are in heaven—where love abounds—so that on Judgment Day, the question will be whether we fit in: On that day, will God know that I am a person who belongs in a family that practices pure and unadulterated love?

Much Scripture in the next chapter provides additional understanding of God's expectations of how we are to love.

The Power of Love

We should not underestimate the power of love, even in the small gestures. While at the University of California San Diego hospital, my wife, Tamara, was being taken care of by a sweet nurse named Brenda who worked through a difficult situation. Tamara had so much scar tissue from PICC lines (a port that allows ease of access for IVs) previously inserted in her veins that installing a new one could only be done on camera, locating it in real time. It took about an hour of tedious concentration to finally find an unfettered vein that was large enough to accept a PICC line. Just before Brenda walked away after the procedure, Tamara, in a very weakened state and without saying a word, took Brenda's hand, looked into her eyes, moved her hand to her lips, and kissed it very gently. I looked at Brenda, and her head sank just a little as she melted with compassion.

Tamara was transferred to a hospital in Nashville the next day. Several days later, Brenda told me that she could not get Tamara off her mind even though she was with her only a short time; she had developed a real love for her. The need to love and be loved nourishes our entire being, our soul. It uplifts us and heals many emotional scars.

Love is powerful in various forms. The following are three examples of its power. The first is from *A Scandalous Freedom* by Steve Brown:

> I was not the best student in the large high school I attended. In fact, I graduated fourth from the bottom in my class. But let me tell you about a teacher who cried when she gave me a low grade on a test. It really surprised me because I generally considered teachers the enemy.
>
> This teacher returned our test papers and asked me to wait after class for mine. I figured I was in really big trouble. After everyone had left, she handed me my paper with a big F marked on it. "Stephen," she said, "you can do a whole lot better than this." And then she started weeping.
>
> I didn't know what to say or how to react. So I quietly left the classroom. Do you know something? I made an A on the next test. I didn't make that A because I had grown smarter or because I bought into academic excellence. I'm not that smart and, at that age, didn't care an ounce about academic excellence. I made an A because a teacher loved me enough to shed tears over my failure. (Brown, 16)

The second example of the power of love is from my son, John-Michael, when he was about four years old. His mother became very irritated by him jumping up and down on the bed on which she was lying. She loudly yelled "Joohnn-Michael," dragging out his name with emphasis. He immediately stopped, dropped to his knees, put one little hand on one of her cheeks, the other little hand on the other, and brought his little face within about five inches of hers and said with a soft voice, "What's wrong, sweetheart?" The tense muscles in her face turned to butter, and the warmth from John-Michael's soft-spoken, loving words melted her all over the sheets. I have never witnessed such a complete and immediate dismantlement and discharge of anger and frustration. It was hilarious!

I have since referred to his ingenious handling of the situation by my four-year-old as "the John-Michael move," and I have learned to use versions of it in my social life and even at work. If someone is angry or frustrated at me, I can attempt to win with a logical and eloquent explanation for my actions or inactions. Or I can simply look at the person with compassion and say, "I am so sorry. I didn't mean to hurt you." Of course, I must mean it for it to be effective. I don't even have to admit that I was wrong; loving words, especially those steeped in compassion, inject a dose of healing antidote to neutralize bitterness, which is much more effective than trying to establish who's right or wrong. If I've matured to a healthy level of selflessness, I won't care who's right or wrong anyway. Also, the mere act itself softens my own heart and opens my mind to feel what that person is feeling. God wants me to feel what others feel, to mourn when they mourn, to the point that I get inside of them.

In the example of the teacher crying over Steve Brown's paper, she got inside him, and her loving words flowed from that perspective. In the next example, you will see that "Wild Bill" got inside of others, which not only helped them, but actually gave him energy and strength. With love, everybody wins, both mentally and physically. The following is his story, which is the third example of the power of love. It is from the book *Return from Tomorrow* by George G. Ritchie, and is his experience at a concentration camp near Wuppertal, Germany. World War II had just ended, and Mr. Ritchie was sent to the camp to help the newly released soldiers who had been held captive for years.

Now I needed my new insight indeed. When the ugliness became too great to handle, I did what I had learned to do. I went from one end to the other of that barbed wire enclosure, looking into men's faces until I saw looking back at me the face of Christ.

And that is how I came to know Wild Bill [Hickok]. That was not his real name. His real name was seven unpronounceable syllables in Polish, but he had a long, drooping handlebar mustache like pictures of the old western hero, so the American soldiers called him Wild Bill. He was one of the inmates of the concentration camp, but obviously he had not been there long: his posture was erect, his eyes bright, his energy indefatigable. Since he was fluent in English, French, German and Russian, as well as Polish, he became a kind of unofficial camp translator.

We came to him with all sorts of problems; the paperwork alone was staggering in attempting to relocate people whose families, even whole hometowns, might have disappeared. But though Wild Bill worked fifteen and sixteen hours a day, he showed no signs of weariness. While the rest of us were drooping with fatigue, he seemed to gain strength. "We have time for this old fellow," he would say. "He's been waiting to see us all day." His compassion for his fellow prisoners glowed on his face, and it was to this glow that I came when my own spirits were low.

So I was astonished to learn, when Wild Bill's own papers came before us one day, that he had been in Wuppertal since 1939! For six years he had lived on the same starvation diet, slept in the same airless and disease-ridden barracks as everyone else, but without the least physical or mental deterioration.

Perhaps even more amazing, every group in the camp looked on him as a friend. He was the one to whom quarrels between inmates were brought for arbitration. Only after I had been at Wuppertal a number of weeks did I realize what a rarity this was in a compound where the different nationalities of prisoners hated each other almost as much as they did the Germans.

As for Germans, feeling against them ran so high that in some of the camps liberated earlier, former prisoners had seized guns, run into the nearest village and simply shot the first Germans they saw. Part of our instructions were to prevent this kind of thing, and again Wild Bill was our greatest asset, reasoning with the different groups, counseling forgiveness.

"It's not easy for some of them to forgive," I commented to him one day as we sat over mugs of tea in the processing center. "So many of them have lost members of their families."

Wild Bill leaned back in the upright chair and sipped at his drink. "We lived in the Jewish section of Warsaw," he began slowly, the first words I had heard him speak about himself, "my wife, our two daughters, and our three little boys. When the Germans reached our street they lined everyone against a wall and opened up with machine guns. I begged to be allowed to die with my family, but because I spoke German they put me in a work group."

He paused, perhaps seeing again his wife and five children. "I had to decide right then," he continued, "whether to let myself hate the soldiers who had done this. It was an easy decision, really. I was a lawyer. In my practice I had seen too often what hate could do to people's minds and bodies. Hate had just killed the six people who mattered most to me in the world. I decided then that I would spend the rest of my life—whether it was a few days or many years—loving every person I came in contact with." (Ritchie, 129–31)

"Love never fails" (1 Corinthians 13:8).

~ 8 ~

What Is the Will of God?

We learned in chapter 5 that to go to heaven, we must do the will of God. God commanded us to live in love for Him (chapter 7), as expressed through obedience, almost entirely as expressed through our love for others, almost entirely as expressed through giving to and caring for others, which we will learn about in this chapter. In the next chapter, we will learn that, after our minds are transformed through the sanctifying work of the Holy Spirit, our loving deeds will flow freely and naturally. We will not view God's will as burdensome but will graciously seek to follow it.

In addition to forgiving and not judging others, which is covered in chapter 10, and Scriptures in chapter 7, carrying out the will of God generally falls into the categories listed below.

> After our minds are transformed through the sanctifying work of the Holy Spirit, our loving deeds will flow freely and naturally. We will not view God's will as burdensome but will graciously seek to follow it.

- Obey the commandments.
- Love and do for others.
- Do not boast about your deeds or expect anything in return.
- Control your internal self.
- Submit to the governing authorities.
- Tithe.

- Worship the Lord your God.
- Lead others to Christ.
- Do not be bound by man-made rules.

In this chapter, we will take a closer look at each of these categories of the Lord's will. But first, I want to draw special attention to the following Scripture, which is not exclusive to one category, but encompasses precepts contained in many of them.

> *Love must be sincere. Hate what is evil; cling to what is good. Be devoted to one another in brotherly love. Honor one another above yourselves. Never be lacking in zeal, but keep your spiritual fervor, serving the Lord. Be joyful in hope, patient in affliction, faithful in prayer. Share with God's people who are in need. Practice hospitality. Bless those who persecute you; bless and do not curse. Rejoice with those who rejoice; mourn with those who mourn. Live in harmony with one another. Do not be proud, but be willing to associate with people of low position. Do not be conceited.* (Romans 12:9–16)

This contains a lot of beauty, and within its small package is a great deal of how we are to live as Christians. It deserves multiple readings.

Obey the Commandments

To enter eternal life, we are to obey the commandments: *"Now a man came up to Jesus and asked, 'Teacher, what good thing must I do to get eternal life?' 'Why do you ask me about what is good?' Jesus replied. 'There is only One who is good. If you want to enter life, obey the commandments'"* (Matthew 19:16–17; see Mark 10:17–19; Luke 18:18–19). *"'Which ones?' the man inquired. Jesus replied, 'Do not murder, do not commit adultery, do not steal, do not give false testimony, honor your father and mother, and love your neighbor as yourself'"* (Matthew 19:18–19). Mark's version states: *"You know the commandments: 'Do not murder, do not commit adultery, do not steal, do not give false testimony, do not defraud, honor your father and mother'"* (Mark 10:19). And Luke states: *"You know the commandments: 'Do not commit adultery, do not murder, do not steal, do not give false testimony, honor your father and mother'"* (Luke 18:20).

It is interesting that when Jesus gave examples of "the commandments" the man was to follow, He did not name all of the Ten Commandments, and He included *"love your neighbor as yourself"* (Matthew 19:19) and *"do not defraud"* (Mark 10:19), neither of which is included in the Ten Commandments. Jesus did not tell this man to obey *all* commandments of the Old Testament, which are in addition to the Ten Commandments. He also did not instruct him to obey the greatest commandment: *"Love the Lord your God with all your heart and with all your soul and with all your mind. This is the first and greatest commandment"* (Matthew 22:37–38).

Why didn't Jesus tell the rich young ruler (he was referred to as being young and with great wealth in Matthew 19:22, of great wealth in Mark 10:22, and a ruler with great wealth in Luke 18:23) to obey the greatest commandment? Could it be that the man acceptably loved God on the surface, but unacceptably loved others, which is the same as unacceptably loving God? Did he hoard his wealth and turn his head from the needs of his fellow man? Did he follow the letter of the law without a full engagement of his heart?

As in other Scriptures, Jesus appears to convey in this story that in our quest to obey the commands of God, we are not to lose our focus on the center of those commands, which is to love, and to love at a high level: As was explained in chapter 7, we cannot pretend to love the Lord our God with all our heart, soul, and mind without loving our neighbor as much as we love ourselves. The apostle Paul confirms that loving others is to be the center of the commands:

> *Let no debt remain outstanding, except the continuing debt to love one another, for he who loves his fellowman has fulfilled the law. The commandments, "Do not commit adultery," "Do not murder," "Do not steal," "Do not covet," and whatever other commandment there may be are* summed up in this one rule: *"Love your neighbor as yourself." Love does no harm to its neighbor. Therefore love is the fulfillment of the law.* (Romans 13:8–10; emphasis added)

The above states that the commandments are summed up in one rule—that we are to love our neighbor as ourselves. It is "the royal law" (James 2:8). The apostle John put it simply: *"And this is his [God's] command: to believe in the name of his Son, Jesus Christ, and to love one another as he commanded us"* (1 John 3:23). The apostle Paul put it even more simply: *"The only thing that counts is faith expressing itself through love"* (Galatians 5:6).

God's commands and those of our Lord Jesus (which are one and the same) are instructions on how we are to love, which are included in this chapter, chapter 7, and chapter 10. Upon being educated by those instructions, we follow our hearts as guided by a good conscience. When we are released from the grip of our sinful nature and are aligned to be in harmony with the Spirit (as instructed in chapter 9), we follow God's commands, not as a burden, but as a fulfillment of our hearts' desire to please Him and to love our fellow man.

Love and Do for Others

Of the instructions given by Jesus, those about loving others were taught most often. The following shows that the call to love is high, and that it is more than conveying words.

> *This is how we know what love is: Jesus Christ laid down his life for us. And we ought to lay down our lives for our brothers. If anyone has material possessions and sees his brother in need but has no pity on him, how can the love of God be in him? Dear children, let us not love with words or tongue but with actions and in truth.* (1 John 3:16–18)

Wow! We ought to *lay down our lives* for others because Jesus laid down His life for us. Let's give that some thought. What if Jesus, before dying, said this to me, face to face: "I will lay down my life for you by dying on the cross, which is the only way for you to go to heaven [John 8:24], if you lay down your life for your brothers." Would I turn my back to that offer, especially if I had just spent a week in heaven and knew firsthand the truth to Jesus' claim that if I knew what it was like, I would, *in my joy*, sell all I have to go there (Matthew 13:44–46)?

By analogy in the parable of the unforgiving servant in Matthew 18:21–35, God did not sacrifice His Son on our promise to obey, but He expects us to obey as though we had. Wouldn't it be easier for us to obey if He *did* require our commitment up front? Perhaps, but a prearranged obligation to obey in return for something is akin to a contractual arrangement, a "business deal" of sorts. Under that arrangement, we would be drawn to keep a mental "scorecard" by measuring Jesus' sacrifice against a growing list of ours, with an eye toward reaching a semblance of equality, the "finish line" of a life of service. We would more likely operate through the head under a commitment to legalism, with less than a full engagement of the heart. Under the new covenant,

God wants a full engagement of our hearts: *"I will put my laws in their minds and write them on their hearts"* (Hebrews 8:10).

We have a continuing debt to love one another, and he who loves his fellow man has fulfilled the law (Romans 13:8). The debt comes with no measuring stick, nor does it have a finish line. Chapter 7 contains a detailed look at Scripture's general principles of loving and making peace with others. Below are a few Scripture passages that show the principles under which we are to express that love:

- *"Do not forget to do good and to share with others, for with such sacrifices God is pleased"* (Hebrews 13:16).
- *"Do nothing out of selfish ambition or conceit, but in humility consider others better than yourselves. Each of you should look not only to your own interests, but to the interests of others"* (Philippians 2:3–4).
- *"Nobody should seek his own good, but the good of others"* (1 Corinthians 10:24).

We cannot carry out effectively the above until we train ourselves to overcome our natural inclination to be self-seeking, which is a path to hell: *"For those who are self-seeking and who reject the truth and follow evil, there will be wrath and anger"* (Romans 2:8). As a society, we undergo little, if any, training to combat and overcome the draw of our self-seeking nature, and as no surprise, we as a society are self-seeking. The training in our lives consists of over a decade up through high school, four years in college for many of us, and for some of us additional years in postgraduate school. With pride and excitement, we receive our diploma in anticipation of it gaining us entrance to a better life here, but it comes with not a scintilla of training to enhance our chances of gaining us entrance to a better life in eternity. Hundreds of television stations bring to our family rooms entertainment and education covering a full gamut of topics, but are virtually void of anything that trains us to be godly. This book is a start in that training: It teaches us to seek the good of others.

Early in my dating relationship with my wife, Tamara, she and I were tailgating with some friends in the parking lot outside of Neyland Stadium at the University of Tennessee, waiting to see the Vols play football. A young lady walked up who knew someone within our group but did not know Tamara or me. Tamara struck up a conversation right away. About ten minutes later, Tamara noticed some dark clouds above, and it became clear that rain would come upon us during the game. The young lady was about to meet a young man who would be her blind date for the game. She had no umbrella or rain jacket. Seeing this, Tamara took off her rain jacket, which had a hood, and told this young lady that she needed to look good for the game. Tamara knew she would be left with neither a rain jacket nor an umbrella and would get drenched.

She sought not her own good, but the good of others. That gesture really warmed my heart. Think about how God felt. One of His children was taking care of one of His children. On that day, Tamara didn't live for herself; she lived for that young lady, someone she didn't even know. *"And he died for all, that those who live should no longer live for themselves but for him who died for them and was raised again"* (2 Corinthians 5:15). Big sacrifices or small, we should live for Jesus, which means to love others through our deeds, even strangers and enemies.

A few years ago, I was blessed by someone who helped me—a complete stranger—when I was in need. I left my office and walked to my car late on a Saturday afternoon, but it would not start because the battery was dead. I called a taxi, and the driver jump-started the battery. He advised me to go to AutoZone, where I could buy a battery and have it installed. I went there, and they had the battery, but no service department. The man behind the counter went outside and opened my hood, and I inquired as to how to change out the battery myself. It was a late-model sports car, and nothing is easy for those cars. It required disassembling a shroud around the battery and working in very tight quarters. Realizing that I obviously was no mechanic, the man said, "If you will be patient with me and allow me to break away as needed to wait on my customers, I will change the battery for you." I was astonished at his kindness, for his computer service report indicated that it was a thirty-minute job, and he didn't know me in the slightest.

He did the work with gladness, and I sensed that he expected nothing in return for his kindness. This man had no idea how much that meant to me. I was in the middle of preparing for an arbitration and was working about eighty hours per week and did not have time to attempt something difficult, especially without proper tools. He knocked it out in fifteen minutes and I compensated him for his effort. He looked at the money, then at me, and with humility said, "That's too much." I said that it was well worth it to me, thanked him wholeheartedly, drove away, and then praised the Lord.

This man set aside his self-centered nature (we all have it) and put the interest of another, a stranger, before himself. Even more impressive, I got the impression that he thought nothing of it and expected nothing in return. His random act of kindness was his light that shone before men (Matthew 5:16).

Let us now delve into the subcategories of the ways in which we are to do for others.

1. We Love Others by Carrying Their Burdens

The apostle Paul wrote, *"Carry each other's burdens, and in this way you will fulfill the law of Christ"* (Galatians 6:2). The following is an example of how to carry the burden of another, even though it is in a very small way.

While sitting at a table at a restaurant after dinner with my seventeen-year-old son on our weekly night out, I noticed that our young waitress was pregnant, and decided to give her a special tip. It then struck me to share a lesson with my son: "Son, did you notice that the young waitress was pregnant? Look at the tip I gave her. It is triple what is customary. I figured she needs the money more than I do." My son responded with excitement, "Dad, I did the exact same thing just the other night for a pregnant waitress!" Boy, did I experience firsthand the love that our God the Father must feel about His children who give to others. I smiled and thanked the Lord that the lessons I had been trying to instill in my son were taking hold. The greatest blessing we can give our children is to teach them by example.

The following shows that we are to carry each others' burdens by giving to those who have little.

> John said to the crowds coming out to be baptized by him, "You brood of vipers! Who warned you to flee from the coming wrath? Produce fruit in keeping with repentance. And do not begin to say to yourselves, 'We have Abraham as our father.' For I tell you that out of these stones God can raise up children for Abraham. The ax is already at the root of the trees, and every tree that does not produce good fruit will be cut down and thrown into the fire."
>
> "What should we do then?" the crowd asked.
>
> John answered, "The man with two tunics should share with him who has none, and the one who has food should do the same."
>
> Tax collectors also came to be baptized. "Teacher," they asked, "what should we do?"

The greatest blessing we can give our children is to teach them by example.

"Don't collect any more than you are required to," he told them.
Then some soldiers asked him, "And what should we do?"
He replied, "Don't extort money and don't accuse people falsely—be
content with your pay." (Luke 3:7–14; cf. Matthew 3:7–10)

To summarize Luke 3:7–14, repentance includes producing fruit, which means to share with those who are without, and to not take money unjustly or make false accusations.

I know a middle-aged lady who lost a lot of income from missing work after having back surgery. As a result, she incurred a debt of $15,200 in credit cards on which she was paying 18–23 percent interest. After paying over $250 per month in interest, plus a certain amount toward the debt, there was very little money left for her basic necessities, for she had a modest income. Until she paid off the debt, which would take three years, she would not be able to buy a house (she lived in an apartment), take a vacation, or splurge on much of anything. She felt strapped, but because of the depth of her character, thoughts of bankruptcy were foreign to her.

A friend of hers became aware of this, and, though he was not wealthy, he had "two tunics" and she had none. To pay off her high-interest credit cards in full, he gave her $6,000 as a gift and loaned her $9,200, which he borrowed at eight percent interest and charged her the same. As a result, her monthly interest payment of $258 was reduced to $61, a difference of $197. That difference was added to the amount she applied monthly to the $9,200 remaining debt, and she was able to pay off her entire debt in eighteen months as opposed to three years.

A heavy burden was lifted off her shoulders. He viewed it as her misfortune that she lost income from back surgery. He was blessed with good health, so he decided to share in her burdens. I can only imagine the pride that welled up in God over that kind deed. One of His children was taking care of one of His children.

Between the gift and the lower-interest loan, she saved approximately $9,000. He, in turn, received from the Lord here on earth more than what he gave up. Also, his heavenly treasure was increased: By being *"generous and willing to share . . . [he] will lay up treasure for [himself] as a firm foundation for the coming age"* (1 Timothy 6:18–19). He and his friend both won. He was operating under the wisdom of the Lord by believing in Scripture and living it. His help in carrying her burdens was contrary to the wisdom of the world, which would have been for him to invest his money for his own benefit. The wisdom of the Lord, the creator of the universe, trumps the wisdom of the world always, especially when it comes to what Scripture says about doing good to others.

As another example, some friends of mine, a married couple, have a cabinet business in Florida. The area was hit hard by the latest real estate downturn, and many cabinet companies had gone out of business during that time. My friends were barely hanging on. Those who had come into their showroom were generally wealthy, and virtually all reminded them of how slow business was for cabinet companies and asked for a discount on the already discounted prices.

God calls us to not conform to the pattern of the world (Romans 12:2) and to carry each other's burdens (Galatians 6:2). Many in a down economy are blessed by the Lord by making as much money as before. What if they, instead of taking advantage of a downturn in the economy, viewed it as an opportunity to help? Imagine a conversation between a customer and a cabinet company owner like this: The owner begins, "Sir, we can provide and install your cabinets for $12,500."

"Does that include a discount based on the competitive market for cabinet companies?" replies the customer.

"Yes, it does," says the owner.

The customer then says, "If this economy were normal, not up or down, how much more would you charge based on an expectation of receiving a reasonable profit?"

"About ten percent more," replies the owner.

The customer's income did not decrease with the downturn, and he happens to know that the owner of this cabinet company is barely hanging on; he views this market as creating an opportunity for himself, not in the wisdom of the world but in the wisdom of God. He smiles and responds by saying, "Then add ten percent to your quote and I'll pay that."

My friends at the cabinet company had been reaching out to the Lord during the time of economic stress. The wife said that, during that time, she turned it all over to Him, agreeing to surrender to His wishes, whether it be to lose the cabinet business or not. Also, she was so excited that her husband, whom she never observed reading the Bible in the past, was reading it on a regular basis. What if the fictitious story above came true and they knew that the customer was a Christian? What a beautiful thing it would be for my friends to see an example of a Christian rising up to the call. As to the customer, I cannot imagine the Lord not blessing him more than the extra ten percent he volunteered to pay.

Everyone wins in this fictitious story: The cabinet company owners are encouraged to go deeper with the Lord because they see the beauty of Christianity in operation. The customer receives joy from what he did, he puts treasure in heaven for himself, and it all comes back to him here, and more.

The last two examples involve sharing money, but those who cannot afford to help financially can find plenty of needs to fulfill by investing their time. In fact, many needs are better fulfilled by offering time. Various ways can be found to share burdens, lend an ear, expose the wounded to the beauty of the Word, and perform other acts of Christianity that cost little or nothing. For a time, I had two roommates who lived at my home at no charge because they fell upon difficult times financially. It didn't cost me anything, we had fruitful conversations about following the Lord, and we developed deeper friendships. The benefits of helping others oftentimes flow both ways.

2. Loving Others Includes Helping Our Relatives

The Bible says, *"If anyone does not provide for his relatives, and especially for his immediate family, he has denied the faith and is worse than an unbeliever"* (1 Timothy 5:8). The Bible gives special attention to widows: *"Give proper recognition to those widows who are really in need. But if a widow has children or grandchildren, these should learn first of all to put their religion into practice by caring for their own family and so repaying their parents and grandparents, for this is pleasing to God"* (1 Timothy 5:3–4). *"If any woman who is a believer has widows in her family, she should help them and not let the church be burdened with them, so that the church can help those widows who are really in need"* (1 Timothy 5:16). As to those who devour widows' houses, a most severe punishment awaits them (Mark 12:40).

I know a man who built a fine home for his family in a nice area of town. After moving in, he felt somewhat guilty because his mother, a widow, lived in a very modest home with an old kitchen that was so small that it was challenging and frustrating for her to prepare a meal. He paid a contractor to tear out the kitchen, move a wall between the kitchen and dining room to make the kitchen bigger, and install new cabinets and appliances. His mother could then cook comfortably, and for the first time in her life, she had a dishwasher. She was in her seventies and would never have had the financial means to have that done. The son shared his wealth with his less fortunate mother.

Are we expected to give to that degree in order to go to heaven? The answer is not in the weight of the gift but in the size of the heart, but the size of the heart is shown by what we give in light of the circumstances. I'm reminded of the story of the poor widow who gave a fraction of a penny in the temple treasury. Jesus said she gave more to the treasury than all the others, which included many rich people who threw in large amounts. Jesus explained that they gave from their wealth, but the lady, out of her poverty, put in everything—all she had to live on (Mark 12:41–44; Luke 21:1–4). Similarly, I know of a man who was barely making ends meet, yet he gave three hundred dollars to his mother because she couldn't make ends meet. One man's circumstances might allow him to pay for remodeling a kitchen without having to give up something for himself, while another might give three hundred dollars at the expense of not having enough to eat. In the eyes of the Lord, which is a larger gift? Because the Lord weighs the heart more than He weighs the gift, it could be that the son who gave three hundred dollars—enabling his mother to pay her bills at a respectable sacrifice to himself—gave even more than the son who gave his mother a kitchen.

After we were married only one year, my wife, Tamara, found out that my stepmother, who was in her late seventies, needed a kidney transplant to live. She immediately volunteered to donate one of her own. As it turns out, the doctors didn't allow it because of incompatibility issues. Nevertheless, Tamara volunteered, without any solicitation from anyone, to undergo surgery, give up a part of her body, be incapacitated for four weeks or more, and run the risk of complications from living with one remaining kidney. What a beautiful act of Christianity.

3. Loving Others Includes Helping the Less Fortunate

We learned in chapter 7 that Jesus taught that when we neglect the less fortunate—those who are hungry, thirsty, without clothes, sick and in prison—we are neglecting Jesus Himself, and in so doing, eternal punishment is our destiny (Matthew 25:41–46).

I heard a story of a man, early in his career and making little, who decided to help his neighbor who was making less. The man went for a long time without lunch because each day he gave his lunch money to his neighbor, who needed it more. Today, the man who sacrificed his lunches for so long is a billionaire, and his life remains centered on giving.

Years ago, an organization in Nashville called Teen Challenge purchased a home to temporarily house teenagers who are addicted to drugs or alcohol. In this home, the teenagers are taught how to break their addiction on a foundation of Christian principles. Teen Challenge is a wonderful program that has a greater than 90 percent success rate and is a beautiful example of fulfilling Jesus' command that we help those in need.

After the purchase, they learned that the zoning regulations did not allow the number of students that they planned to accommodate, so they had to apply for a zoning change. Unfortunately, many of the neighbors rallied to oppose the change under the fear that their property values would decrease if Teen Challenge moved in. How sad it is that Jesus commands us to do much more than undergo a mere risk that our worldly fortunes will be decreased in order to help the less fortunate, yet many of us cannot even do that! We must rid ourselves of selfish thinking.

I know a man who, every Monday, takes about eighty meals and eighty small New Testaments to the homeless. As he and his friends hand them out, he asks if anyone needs prayer. On one occasion in which I helped, I prayed over one of the homeless men. I found out that he had served a prison term of five years and was fearful that a birth certificate would not be received from his home state in time to meet the deadline imposed by law to register himself in Tennessee, where he was residing. If it didn't arrive in time, the homeless man would have to spend an additional ninety days in jail. I got his phone number and promised to help him.

The next day, my legal assistant made some calls to find out how to resolve the situation. The day after that, I picked up the homeless man, brought him to my office, had him fill out paperwork and an affidavit, and then drove him back. My assistant overnighted the paperwork to the vital records department in the man's home state, along with an overnight return package to expedite the return of the birth certificate.

I got such joy out of that. By spending a couple of hours in total and less than fifty dollars, I soaked in the joy of knowing I saved my homeless friend from spending an additional ninety days in jail. Instead of walking away from a man who was guilty of committing a crime, I chose not to judge him but to help him. Later, the man told me that he had been spiritually broken prior to the time I helped him and that he was seeking to get closer to the Lord. My small contribution led my homeless friend to open the door of his soul so that God could do His divine work in him. We are not to judge, but to help many. The Lord will take it from there.

The following offers additional instruction on helping the less fortunate:

- *"When you give a banquet, invite the poor, the crippled, the lame, the blind, and you will be blessed. Although they cannot repay you, you will be repaid at the resurrection of the righteous"* (Luke 14:13–14).
- *"If a man shuts his ears to the cry of the poor, he too will cry out and not be answered"* (Proverbs 21:13).
- *"He who gives to the poor will lack nothing, but he who closes his eyes to them receives many curses"* (Proverbs 28:27).
- *"Encourage the timid, help the weak, be patient with everyone"* (1 Thessalonians 5:14; see Romans 15:1–2).
- *"Religion that God our Father accepts as pure and faultless is this: to look after orphans and widows in their distress and to keep oneself from being polluted by the world"* (James 1:27).

For clarity, no place in the Bible does it call for the government to help the poor or otherwise to facilitate a sharing of wealth. That makes sense, for who would be given credit for doing good deeds?* If politician Paul forces Bob to give to Bill, why would Paul receive credit, for he sacrificed nothing? Why would Bob receive credit, for his payment was mandatory? God calls for us as individuals to give. Not only that, but we are to give from the heart, not under compulsion (2 Corinthians 9:6–8).

Also, those who are being helped should see it as temporary and not become dependent, *"to work with your hands, just as we told you, so that your daily life may win the respect of outsiders and so that you will not be dependent on anybody"* (1 Thessalonians 4:11–12).

4. To Love Others, We "Get Inside" Them

"Keep on loving each other as brothers. Do not forget to entertain strangers, for by so doing some people have entertained angels without knowing it. Remember those in prison as if you were their fellow prisoners, and those who are mistreated as if you yourselves were suffering" (Hebrews 13:1–3). This

---

* Though our motive to give should not be for an expectation of a return, Jesus did speak of credits, repayment, and rewards for those who give, which is pointed out later in this book. The point here is that there is no reason for God to look with favor on anyone by way of government assistance.

Scripture is rich in expectations. Do we consider all people as brothers? This Scripture instructs us to love all as though they were. It also tells us that angels are in our midst. We should, therefore, be extra careful of how we treat everyone. Most importantly, this Scripture tells us that we are to "get inside" other people: We are to remember prisoners as if we were in prison with them, and remember those who suffer as though we are suffering. By feeling their pain, we will be more inclined to help them. It will also make us more effective in knowing and understanding their needs.

I know a man who is in prison awaiting trial on multiple felony charges. His pastor, a woman, visited him, reaching out to a man who was hurting very deeply. She told me that, during the visitation, he held both of her hands with a loving touch and that it was plain to see his hunger for the support of a friend. In Matthew 25:43, Jesus instructed us to look after those in prison, without limitation to only those who are innocent or those who committed less than the most serious crimes. This pastor reached out as a Christian without judging the inmate or deciding whether he deserved her love and compassion. The state will do its part by determining this man's guilt or innocence. We shouldn't. As Christians, we should do our part and visit those in prison, whether we believe in a person's guilt or innocence, and regardless of how heinous we might view the crime.

A landscaper was working on a lot beside mine and I asked how much he would charge to remove a huge bush in my yard that had overgrown to the size of a small tree. He said $100, and I agreed. Upon submitting his invoice, I learned that he paid $100 to a third party to have it hauled off, and therefore he would end up not being paid anything for his labor. From my perspective, a deal is a deal. From his perspective, he got short-changed even though it was his fault.

I offered to pay him $200, and he was very appreciative. If the value to me was no more than $100 and I would not have agreed for him to do the work had his price been more than $100, then I would not feel obligated to pay him more (that is not to say I would not pay him more). But if I were willing to pay him more in the first place, how could I feel good about holding him to his price knowing that he made a mistake? As a construction lawyer and architect for many years, I have known of only one occasion where someone volunteered to pay more than the price given up front. Christian principles should be applied in business the same as in our personal lives.

5. Loving Others Includes Loving and Helping Our Enemies

Special attention should be given to this Scripture passage:

> *Do not repay anyone evil for evil. Be careful to do what is right in the eyes of everybody. If it is possible, as far as it depends on you, live at peace with everyone. Do not take revenge, my friends, but leave room for God's wrath, for it is written: "It is mine to avenge; I will repay," says the Lord. On the contrary:*
>
> *"If your enemy is hungry, feed him; if he is thirsty, give him something to drink. In doing this, you will heap burning coals on his head."*
>
> *Do not be overcome by evil, but overcome evil with good.* (Romans 12:17–21)

Do we allow evil to overcome us, or do we overcome evil with good? It is very difficult sometimes to do good to those who hurt us, but we should be ever mindful of the power of love, which never fails (1 Corinthians 13:8).

> *"Love your enemies, do good to those who hate you, bless those who curse you, pray for those who mistreat you. If someone strikes you on one cheek, turn to him the other also. If someone takes your cloak, do not stop him from taking your tunic. Give to everyone who asks you, and if anyone takes what belongs to you, do not demand it back. Do to others as you would have them do to you."* (Luke 6:27–31)

> *"You have heard that it was said, 'Eye for eye, and tooth for tooth.' But I tell you, Do not resist an evil person. If someone strikes you on the right cheek, turn to him the other also. And if someone wants to sue you and take your tunic, let him have your cloak as well. If someone forces you to go one mile, go with him two miles. Give to the one who asks you, and do not turn away from the one who wants to borrow from you."* (Matthew 5:38–42)

> *"You have heard that it was said, 'Love your neighbor and hate your enemy.' But I tell you: Love your enemies and pray for those who persecute you, that you may be sons of your Father in heaven. He causes his sun to rise on the evil and the good, and sends rain on the righteous and the unrighteous. If you love those who love you, what reward will you get? Are not even the tax collectors doing that? And if you greet only your brothers, what are you doing more than others? Do not even pagans do that? Be perfect, therefore, as your heavenly Father is perfect."* (Matthew 5:43–48)

We feel good about ourselves when we're good to others. But if the "others" are those who are good to us, we get no credit, for even sinners do the same. If, however, we rise to the level of the Most High by doing as God does, which is to be kind to the ungrateful and wicked, then

We feel good about ourselves when we're good to others. But if the "others" are those who are good to us, we get no credit, for even sinners do the same.

our reward will be great. That is so difficult, especially when it is against our nature to be good to our enemies, and we get little encouragement from the worldly ways, for we see few strive to be that way. That is another reason we are to "put our blinders on" and not be corrupted by the ways of the world (2 Peter 2:20), but to strive to be perfect as God is perfect (Matthew 5:48), and to work toward being transformed into His likeness (2 Corinthians 3:18) so that we can *"be imitators of God"* (Ephesians 5:1). Even when we speak, we should do it as one speaking the very words of God (1 Peter 4:11).

I believe that overcoming the battle within us to want to "pay back" our enemies is one of the greatest challenges as Christians. We should remember that the right to avenge is reserved exclusively for the Lord (Leviticus 19:18; Hebrews 10:30), and we are to leave room for His wrath (Romans 12:17–19). He is a much better judge on these matters than we are (Hebrews 10:30). As we mature, when wronged, we escape thoughts of revenge more quickly. Those who are fully mature in God's ways don't allow those thoughts to enter them at all. I believe that few of us have reached full maturity. I haven't, but will continue to work toward it, and pray for the assistance of the sanctifying work of Holy Spirit in that regard.

6. In Loving Others, We Are Not to Show Favoritism

The apostle Paul said we are to do nothing out of favoritism (1 Timothy 5:21). In fact, it is a sin: *"If you really keep the royal law found in Scripture, 'Love your neighbor as yourself,' you are doing right. But if you show favoritism, you sin"* (James 2:8–9). This Scripture tells us that if we show favoritism, we are not loving our neighbor as ourselves. That is consistent with Scripture instructing us to love everyone, including our enemies.

When Jesus told a crowd, "Love your neighbor as yourself" in Luke 10:25–37, someone asked Him who is his neighbor, whereupon Jesus told the parable of the good Samaritan helping a stranger in need. When combining this parable with James 2:8–9, to avoid showing favoritism, those we help should not be limited to those we know.

Two examples are given in the New Testament as to ways in which we are not to show favoritism: Though elders who direct the affairs of the church well are worthy of double honor, especially those whose work is preaching and teaching, the ones who are sinning are to be reproved before everyone, so that others may take warning (1 Timothy 5:17–21); as a second example, we are not to judge a person by outside appearances (James 2:1–4). When we show favoritism by treating those with fine clothes differently from those with tattered old clothes, we have discriminated among ourselves and become judges with evil thoughts. None of us want to be judged, largely because it is almost always based on a lack of information. In fact, we are not to judge at all (see chapter 10).

We need to be careful not to take the instruction not to show favoritism too far: We all have favorites with whom we enjoy spending our time, and we are more inclined to help those close to us. As to all of God's commands, we carry them out with wisdom, with common sense, and with love in our hearts.

7.   Loving Others Includes Sharing All Good Things with Our Instructors

"Anyone who receives instruction in the word must share all good things with his instructor" (Galatians 6:6). This includes paying preachers: *"The Lord has commanded that those who preach the gospel should receive their living from the gospel"* (1 Corinthians 9:14; see 1 Timothy 5:17–18; see also Romans 15:27). For the rationale for paying those who preach, see 1 Corinthians 9:7–12.

We should gladly reward our ministers with a deserved salary. We also should not neglect the needs of those who help to bring us closer to the Lord through instruction of the Word, whether or not it is done through a church. We should inquire as to their needs, and seek to fulfill them.

8.   In Loving Others, We Are to Be Proactive in Seeking Ways to Do for Them

The apostle James proclaimed that we are to be proactive: *"Anyone, then, who knows the good he ought to do and doesn't do it, sins"* (James 4:17).

Therefore, we are called to do more than simply do the right thing when confronted with something. If we choose to do nothing when there is something good that we ought to do, that is a sin. In other words, sins are more than sins of commission—they include sins of omission.

Each day, we can look around and find all kinds of good to do, such as help someone who lost a job to find another one and, if needed, give

Sins are more than sins of commission— they include sins of omission.

financial assistance; we can reach out to befriend someone who is lonely; we can go to the grocery store for someone who's sick and living alone; we can mow the lawn of an elderly couple who cannot afford to pay someone; we can invite a man to meet for coffee whose wife just left him and provide a safe place to vent his pain; we can invite individuals without family in town to our own family Thanksgiving dinner; and we can try to bring peace to a hostile situation. The possibilities for doing good are endless.

While at my office early one morning, I heard a loud car crash. It was in the direction of a fairly busy street, and I was sure that many would be there to give it proper attention, so I went back to my work. A few seconds later, however, I thought that perhaps I should check on the situation just in case. Was there some good I ought to do here? (James 4:17).

I hurried to my car and drove in the direction where I heard the crash. An older-model car had run off the road and crashed head-on into a tree. I pulled over, got out, and ran to the wreckage and found an elderly lady by herself in the driver's seat. A few people had pulled over, and one was calling an ambulance. As I approached the car, I could see that the lady's lip had begun to swell a great deal. She looked at me and, with distant eyes that looked as though she was in a state of shock, said, "I don't know what happened." I told her I would get some ice for her lip and be right back.

I drove quickly back to my office, threw some ice in a plastic storage bag, and then rushed back to her. An ambulance had arrived, but they had no ice. I could see the comfort and appreciation in her eyes when I handed her the bag of ice. I asked if I could pray for her, and she eagerly nodded her head. I held her hand while asking the Lord to bring her healing and a sense of calm, and I asked for the Lord's protection over her in every way. She squeezed my hand at the end of the prayer and I left, not to get in the way of the paramedics.

My heart was joyful upon leaving, knowing that I might have made a slight difference in her day, not just by helping relieve the pain of her swollen lip, but hopefully by giving her comfort through prayer. It was such a small sacrifice on my part, and I probably received as much joy from it as did she.

We should never pass up an opportunity to let our light shine before men, so that they can see our good deeds—even the little ones— and praise our Father in heaven (Matthew 5:16). In fact, we are called to *"make the most of every opportunity"* (Colossians 4:5).

We have a high calling to be proactive. We are to work not just for ourselves, but so that we have more than we need in order to share with others: *"He who has been stealing must steal no longer, but must work, doing something useful with his own hands, that he may have something to share with those in need"* (Ephesians 4:28). The apostle Paul said, *"You yourselves know that these hands of mine have supplied my own needs and the needs of my companions. In everything I did, I showed you that by this kind of hard work we must help the weak, remembering the words the Lord Jesus himself said: 'It is more blessed to give than to receive'"* (Acts 20:34–35).

If we choose to do nothing to help others, we face grave consequences, as the writer of Hebrews warns: *"Land that drinks in the rain often falling on it and that produces a crop useful to those for whom it is farmed receives the blessing of God. But land that produces thorns and thistles is worthless and is in danger of being cursed. In the end, it will be burned. Even though we speak like this, dear friends, we are confident of better things in your case—things that accompany salvation. God is not unjust; he will not forget your work and the love you have shown him as you have helped his people and continue to help them"* (Hebrews 6:7–10).

We are to work not just for ourselves, but so that we have more than we need in order to share with others.

In describing what the kingdom of heaven will be like, Jesus tells the following parable to illustrate that if we are lazy servants, we will be thrown into the darkness, where there will be weeping and gnashing of teeth:

> *Again, it [the kingdom of heaven] will be like a man going on a journey, who called his servants and entrusted his property to them. To one he gave five talents of money, to another two talents, and to another one talent, each according to his ability. Then he went on his journey. The man who had received the five talents went at once and put his money to work*

and gained five more. So also, the one with the two talents gained two more. But the man who had received the one talent went off, dug a hole in the ground and hid his master's money.

After a long time the master of those servants returned and settled accounts with them. The man who had received the five talents brought the other five. "Master," he said, "you entrusted me with five talents. See, I have gained five more."

His master replied, "Well done, good and faithful servant! You have been faithful with a few things; I will put you in charge of many things. Come and share your master's happiness!"

The man with the two talents also came. "Master," he said, "you entrusted me with two talents; see, I have gained two more."

His master replied, "Well done, good and faithful servant! You have been faithful with a few things; I will put you in charge of many things. Come and share your master's happiness!"

Then the man who had received the one talent came. "Master," he said, "I knew that you are a hard man, harvesting where you have not sown and gathering where you have not scattered seed. So I was afraid and went out and hid your talent in the ground. See, here is what belongs to you."

His master replied, "You wicked, lazy *servant! So you knew that I harvest where I have not sown and gather where I have not scattered seed? Well then, you should have put my money on deposit with the bankers, so that when I returned I would have received it back with interest. Take the talent from him and give it to the one who has the ten talents. For everyone who has will be given more, and he will have an abundance. Whoever does not have, even what he has will be taken from him. And throw that* worthless servant *outside, into the darkness, where there will be weeping and gnashing of teeth."* (Matthew 25:14–30; emphasis added)

In this parable, three people are given different amounts of money ("talents"), each according to his ability. These varying amounts of money represent varying assignments, whether in quantity or weight. Those who have greater abilities are given greater assignments. We are to use our assignments to the best of our abilities to advance the interest of the master, God.

The man with one talent hid it in the ground because he "was afraid." The master called him lazy and wicked and said that he should have at least put the money on deposit with the bankers, which would have been safe. In other words, the servant did nothing, not because of his proclaimed fear, but because he was lazy, because there should be nothing to fear in depositing money in a bank. Therefore, we are to carry out our tasks to the best of our abilities, without excuse.

The following is Frederick Dale Bruner's insight when synthesizing this parable with the Scripture regarding the Lord saying that *"whatever you did not do for the least of these you did not do for me"* (Matthew 25:45):

> This teaching remarkably parallels the main teaching of the preceding parable—of the one-talented servant who was judged because he did nothing with his master's gift (v. 18). Matthew's Jesus seeks through this double teaching to move disciples into "immediate" (v. 16) helping. Not to feed a hungry man is to kill him. Not to care for persons' basic needs, in the name perhaps of a supposedly priority evangelism, not to think that other people's problems are our problems under the banner of "charity begins at home" or of a rugged individualism, not to be there when people need us—all these nullities are what damn in Jesus' teaching. Thus disciples who in good faith hear this "Damnation of nothings" will fall on their knees in poverty of spirit to ask the Lord to give them another chance to be something the rest of their lives—however inadequate, however little, however basic—to the persons they are given. (Bruner, 2:927)

This is in keeping with the apostle Paul's instructing us to warn those who are idle (1 Thessalonians 5:14). Consider another parable which calls for an even higher level of proactive service:

> *Suppose one of you had a servant plowing or looking after the sheep. Would he say to the servant when he comes in from the field, "Come along now and sit down to eat"? Would he not rather say, "Prepare my supper, get yourself ready and wait on me while I eat and drink; after that you may eat and drink"? Would he thank the servant because he did what he was told to do? So you also, when you have done everything you were told to do, should say, "We are* unworthy *servants; we have only done our duty."* (Luke 17:7–10; emphasis added)

Therefore, we are not to simply wait for opportunities to do the work of the Lord. We are to seek them out. Perhaps we should also pray to God to bring us people who need us so we can be of service to them.

I was told a wonderful story about a small town in America. The men of the town invite widows to post on the community center bulletin board their requests for repairs on their respective houses and other chores that are difficult for them. The men view the bulletin board and volunteer their time to help those widows. What a beautiful example of Christianity. Those men are being proactive in producing fruit: They are utilizing their talents to help others and are sharing in the burdens of others.

In summary of this section, "Love and Do for Others," we must proactively seek to do good deeds (Ephesians 4:28; Matthew 25:14–30). In fact, we must do more than our duty, for if we do only our duty, we are unworthy servants (Luke 17:7–10). We must turn from our natural inclination to be self-seeking (Romans 2:8) and turn from our ways of selfish ambition (Philippians 2:3–4). We are to help the least of our brothers (Matthew 25:41–46), bear with the failings of the weak (Romans 15:1–2), help the weak (1 Thessalonians 5:14), entertain strangers (Hebrews 13:2), help our enemies (Romans 12:17–21), help orphans and widows (James 1:27), provide for our relatives, especially for our immediate family (1 Timothy 5:8), not show favoritism (1 Timothy 5:21; James 2:8–9), share all good things with our instructor (Galatians 6:6), share our material possessions with those in need (Luke 3:7–14; 1 John 3:17–18), carry the burdens of others (Galatians 6:1), practice hospitality, live in harmony, associate with people of low position (Romans 12:13–16), and invite the poor to our banquets (Luke 14:12–14). In all this, if we know the good we ought to do and don't do it, we are sinning (James 4:17).

We are not to simply wait for opportunities to do the work of the Lord. We are to seek them out.

All the above are high expectations of us, but we are not to become weary in doing good, for the harvest will come at the proper time, but only if we do not give up (Galatians 6:9).

Do Not Boast About Your Deeds or Expect Anything in Return

"Let your light shine before men, that they may see your good deeds and praise your Father in heaven" (Matthew 5:16). Jesus tells us here to allow others

to see our good deeds, yet He also cautions us not to do our acts of
service to be seen by others:

> *"Be careful not to do your 'acts of righteousness' before men, to be seen*
> *by them. If you do, you will have no reward from your Father in heaven. So*
> *when you give to the needy, do not announce it with trumpets, as the hypo-*
> *crites do in the synagogues and on the streets, to be honored by men. I tell*
> *you the truth, they have received their reward in full. But when you give to*
> *the needy, do not let your left hand know what your right hand is doing, so*
> *that your giving may be in secret. Then your Father, who sees what is done*
> *in secret, will reward you."* (Matthew 6:1–4)

How do we reconcile Matthew 5:16 with Matthew 6:1–4? Jesus is admonishing us to be careful as to our motives. When we give, is it for
appearance or out of a sincere desire to help others? Do we desire that
God get the praise, or that we do? It is the heart behind the gift that
matters.

By all means, if we announce a plan to help others, we should not
fail to follow through. A famous man announced in the mid-1990s that
he would give away $1 billion to charity. I read that he gave away a large
percentage of it, but that he did not follow through with his announced
commitment. A few years later, I read that his net worth decreased by
approximately 90 percent. Did God cause that? I don't know, but it
must be very displeasing to God to invite praise to oneself by announc-
ing a promise of good deeds but not following through.

Jesus taught that when we give, we are to expect nothing in return:

- *"Jesus said to his host, 'When you give a luncheon or dinner, do not invite*
  your friends, your brothers or relatives, or your rich neighbors; if you do,
  they may invite you back and so you will be repaid. But when you give a
  banquet, invite the poor, the crippled, the lame, the blind, and you will
  be blessed. Although they cannot repay you, you will be repaid *at the*
  resurrection of the righteous'" (Luke 14:12–14; emphasis added).
- *"If you love those who love you,* what credit is that to you? *Even 'sin-*
  ners' love those who love them. And if you do good to those who are good
  to you, what credit is that to you? *Even 'sinners' do that. And if you*
  lend to those from whom you expect repayment, what credit is that
  to you? Even 'sinners' lend to 'sinners,' expecting to be repaid in full"
  (Luke 6:32–34; emphasis added).

- *"If you love those who love you,* what reward will you get? *Are not even the tax collectors doing that? And if you greet only your brothers, what are you doing more than others? Do not even pagans do that?"* (Matthew 5:46–47; emphasis added).
- *Love your enemies, do good to them, and lend to them without expecting to get anything back.* Then *your reward will be great, and you will be sons of the Most High, because he is kind to the ungrateful and wicked"* (Luke 6:35; emphasis added).

Do you see the commonality of the emphasized words above (shown by regular type)? It's as though the gap in the balance sheet between what we give and what we receive ascends as our treasure to heaven, awaiting our arrival.

Control Your Internal Self

The following illustrates the acts of the sinful nature, and that which manifests itself when we follow the Spirit:

> *The acts of the sinful nature are obvious: sexual immorality, impurity and debauchery; idolatry and witchcraft; hatred, discord, jealousy, fits of rage, selfish ambition, dissensions, factions, and envy; drunkenness, orgies, and the like. I warn you as I did before, that those who live like this* will not inherit the kingdom of God.
> *But the fruit of the Spirit is love, joy, peace, patience, kindness, goodness, faithfulness, gentleness and self-control. Against such things there is no law. Those who belong to Christ Jesus have crucified the sinful nature with its passions and desires. Since we live by the Spirit, let us keep in step with the Spirit.* (Galatians 5:19–25; emphasis added)

As stated above and in Romans 8:13, those of us who live according to the sinful nature will die. The acts of the sinful nature are stated in the first paragraph above; they are clear and require no explanation.

As to sexual immorality, it is one of the most challenging acts to avoid, especially because of the influence of the ways of the world. It is easy to try to justify behavior by protesting that "it's what everyone else is doing." We cannot fall into a false sense of security in believing that God would not judge as sexually immoral that which is accepted by the majority. That is when we should look to Scripture that admonishes us not to be polluted by the world and to overcome the world. We also shouldn't try to justify our behavior under the pretense that acts of two consenting adults are not hurting anyone. We don't always know God's reasons behind his commands, but we don't have to know; we simply must obey.

> *The body is not meant for sexual immorality, but for the Lord, and the Lord for the body. By his power God raised the Lord from the dead, and he will raise us also. Do you not know that your bodies are members of Christ himself? Shall I then take the members of Christ and unite them with a prostitute? Never! Do you not know that he who unites himself with a prostitute is one with her in body? For it is said, "The two will become one flesh." But he who unites himself with the Lord is one with him in spirit.*
>
> *Flee from sexual immorality. All other sins a man commits are outside his body, but he who sins sexually sins against his own body. Do you not know that your body is a temple of the Holy Spirit, who is in you, whom you have received from God? You are not your own; you were bought at a price. Therefore honor God with your body.* (1 Corinthians 6:13–20)

As followers of Christ, we do not own our bodies—Christ does. I picture myself at times "stepping out" of my body and telling God to come in and completely control me. That makes it a little easier to avoid temptation. I tell myself I have no control, no choice—I cannot sin because the seed of God is in me (1 John 3:9). This exercise does not keep me free from sin, for we all sin, but it can be a method to help step away from temptations.

The Bible has more to say on self-control and internal goodness:

- *"In a similar way, Sodom and Gomorrah and the surrounding towns gave themselves up to sexual immorality and perversion. They serve as an example of those who suffer the punishment of eternal fire"* (Jude 1:7).
- *"The cowardly, the unbelieving, the vile, the murderers, the sexually immoral, those who practice magic arts, the idolaters and all liars—their place will be in the fiery lake of burning sulfur"* (Revelation 21:8).
- *"Nothing impure will ever enter it, nor will anyone who does what is shameful or deceitful, but only those whose names are written in the Lamb's book of life"* (Revelation 21:27).
- *"Among you there must not be even a hint of sexual immorality, or of any kind of impurity, or of greed, because these are improper for God's holy people. Nor should there be obscenity, foolish talk or coarse joking, which*

are out of place, but rather thanksgiving. For of this you can be sure: No immoral, impure or greedy person—such a man is an idolater—has any inheritance in the kingdom of Christ and of God. Let no one deceive you with empty words, for because of such things God's wrath comes on those who are disobedient. Therefore do not be partners with them" (Ephesians 5:3–7).

- *"He has condemned the great prostitute who corrupted the earth by her adulteries"* (Revelation 19:2).
- A divisive person *"is warped and sinful; he is self-condemned"* (Titus 3:10–11).
- *"Do you not know that the wicked will not inherit the kingdom of God? Do not be deceived: Neither the sexually immoral nor idolaters nor adulterers nor male prostitutes nor homosexual offenders nor thieves nor the greedy nor drunkards nor slanderers nor swindlers will inherit the kingdom of God"* (1 Corinthians 6:9–10).
- *"Put to death, therefore, whatever belongs to your earthly nature: sexual immorality, impurity, lust, evil desires and greed, which is idolatry. Because of these, the wrath of God is coming. You used to walk in these ways, in the life you once lived. But now you must rid yourselves of all such things as these: anger, rage, malice, slander, and filthy language from your lips. Do not lie to each other, since you have taken off your old self with its practices and have put on the new self, which is being renewed in knowledge in the image of its Creator"* (Colossians 3:5–10).

Self-control includes controlling our tongue:

- *"If anyone considers himself religious and yet does not keep a tight rein on his tongue, he deceives himself and his religion is worthless"* (James 1:26).
- *"With the tongue we praise our Lord and Father, and with it we curse men, who have been made in God's likeness. Out of the same mouth come praise and cursing. My brothers, this should not be"* (James 3:9–10).
- *"Make a tree good and its fruit will be good, or make a tree bad and its fruit will be bad, for a tree is recognized by its fruit. You brood of vipers, how can you who are evil say anything good? For out of the overflow of the heart the mouth speaks. The good man brings good things out of the good stored up in him, and the evil man brings evil things out of the evil stored up in him. But I tell you that men will have to give account on the day of judgment for every careless word they have spoken. For by your words you will be acquitted, and by your words you will be condemned"* (Matthew 12:33–37).

Jesus said in this Scripture that the good man brings good things out of the good stored up in him and that out of the overflow of the heart, the mouth speaks. If our speech is cleansed at its source—that is, if we live in accordance with the Spirit and allow the Holy Spirit to assist us in changing our ways—the words that flow from our mouths will clean up on their own. This is one of the biggest changes that has occurred to me since losing my wife. When treated unfairly or harshly, I am slower to anger. I no longer speak harsh words except for when I slip occasionally; hateful thoughts have virtually left me, and when they occasionally come to me, I ask the Lord for understanding and strength to set them aside. I still become angry, but rarely as to injustices inflicted on me and almost exclusively over injustices inflicted on others. I have angry thoughts over the source of those injustices, but not hateful thoughts. It is no surprise that because the source of my words is cleaner, my words are cleaner.

How did this change come over me? I learned to change my perception: Instead of quickly condemning a person for offensive acts, I now see him as a probable victim of improper teaching and training that tarnished his mind, from which the offensive acts were directed. Thus, I try to judge the improper teaching and training, not the person, to be the true source of the unjust act. Not only does that new way of thinking help me escape anxiety and anger that comes naturally if I knew only to take offense and react rather than to understand, but I am more likely to search for a way to help that person overcome his obstacles. With a compassionate heart as my aid, which comes from understanding, and a desire to love my neighbor as myself, which comes from spiritual maturity, I seek to know the stained underlying source of the offensive acts. If the opportunity presents itself, I try to approach the person with subtle words about the sanctifying power of the Holy Spirit and hopefully bring him to tap into that power—through following the Word—so that the person may be cleansed at the source and reverse the effect that past improper training and teaching had on him.

This is not to say that a stern reprimand is not also in order, which can be a necessary part of training, but even that should be done from a heart of compassion, not a condemning heart. This whole approach is easier said than done, and I have to remind myself, when faced with an injustice, to think and act, not react. It remains a work in progress.

You, man of God, flee from all this, and pursue righteousness, godliness, faith, love, endurance and gentleness. Fight the good fight of the faith.

Take hold of the eternal life to which you were called when you made your good confession in the presence of many witnesses. (1 Timothy 6:11–12)

In summary of this subtopic, "Control Your Internal Self," if we belong to Christ Jesus, we have crucified the sinful nature with its passions and desires, which includes the following acts: sexual immorality, impurity and debauchery; idolatry and witchcraft; hatred, discord, jealousy, fits of rage, selfish ambition, dissensions, factions, and envy; and drunkenness and orgies (Galatians 5:19–21). We are not to be perverted (Jude 1:7), shameful or deceitful (Revelation 21:27), nor are we to be involved with obscenity, foolish talk or coarse joking (Ephesians 5:4). We are not to be cowardly, unbelieving, vile, murderers, practitioners of magic arts, or liars (Revelation 21:8). We are not to be adulterers, prostitutes, homosexual offenders, thieves, slanderers, or swindlers (1 Corinthians 6:9–10). We must put to death evil desires and greed, which is idolatry (Colossians 3:5). We are to rid ourselves of anger, rage, malice, slander, and filthy language (Colossians 3:8). We are to be careful with our words (Matthew 12:33–37). And we must pursue righteousness, godliness, faith, love, endurance, and gentleness (1 Timothy 6:11–12).

Submit to the Governing Authorities

As shown by the following Scriptures, submitting to the governing authorities serves multiple purposes.

"Obey your leaders and submit to their authority. Obey them so that their work will be a joy, not a burden, for that would be of no advantage to you" (Hebrews 13:17). We are not to be a burden on others; in fact, we are to carry each other's burdens (Galatians 6:2).

"Submit yourselves for the Lord's sake to every authority instituted among men: whether to the king, as the supreme authority, or to governors, who are sent by him to punish those who do wrong and to commend those who do right. For it is God's will that by doing good you should silence the ignorant talk of foolish men. Live as free men, but do not use your freedom as a cover-up for evil; live as servants of God. Show proper respect to everyone: Love the brotherhood of believers, fear God, honor the king" (1 Peter 2:13–17). We carry the badge of Christianity, and by our acts, we are to give honor to the name.

"The Lord knows how to rescue godly men from trials and to hold the unrighteous for the day of judgment, while continuing their punishment. This is

especially true of those who follow the corrupt desire of the sinful nature and spise authority" (2 Peter 2:9–10; emphasis added). Here on earth, we learn not to despise authority, but to respect it; that mindset will make it easier to respect God as the authority in heaven, so that, as stated in the Lord's Prayer, His will can be done there.

"*Everyone must submit himself to the governing authorities, for there is no authority except that which God has established. The authorities that exist have been established by God. Consequently, he who rebels against the authority is rebelling against what God has instituted, and those who do so will bring judgment on themselves. For rulers hold no terror for those who do right, but for those who do wrong. Do you want to be free from fear of the one in authority? Then do what is right and he will commend you. For he is God's servant to do you good. But if you do wrong, be afraid, for he does not bear the sword for nothing. He is God's servant, an agent of wrath to bring punishment on the wrongdoer*" (Romans 13:1–4). This, in addition to fulfilling God's plan for justice here (Psalm 9:16), has a higher purpose—to discipline us for our own good, and doing so produces a harvest of righteousness and peace for those who have been trained by it (Hebrews 12:10–11). Therefore, the governing authorities, being agents of God's wrath, could very well play a role in the conversion process, especially to those of us who need an extra measure of discipline. Those in positions of authority should realize the seriousness of their roles, especially judges, for they are agents for the Lord in bringing justice, which is shown multiple times in the Bible to be of great importance to the Lord and in turning men and women from the error of their ways (James 5:19–20).

Tithe

Jesus said, "*Give to Caesar what is Caesar's, and to God what is God's*" (Matthew 22:21). Obviously, this instructs us to submit to the governing authorities by paying taxes, and it instructs us to tithe. Jesus indirectly tells us in Matthew 23:23 that "what is God's" is ten percent of our income: "*Woe to you, teachers of the law and Pharisees, you hypocrites! You give a tenth of your spices—mint, dill and cummin. But you have neglected the more important matters of the law—justice, mercy and faithfulness. You should have practiced the latter without neglecting the former.*" Deuteronomy 14:22 is clear that we are to tithe ten percent. In fact, ten percent of our income belongs to the Lord (Leviticus 27:30–32). Therefore, ten

:r ours in the first place. God is so serious about the
cent of what we receive is His money that He declared
g it over is robbing Him:

n to me, and I will return to you," says the LORD Almighty.
⌐ you ask, 'How are we to return?'
"Will a man rob God? Yet you rob me.
"But you ask, 'How do we rob you?'
"In tithes and offerings. You are under a curse—the whole nation of
you—because you are robbing me. Bring the whole tithe into the store-
house, that there may be food in my house. Test me in this," says the LORD
Almighty, "and see if I will not throw open the floodgates of heaven and
pour out so much blessing that you will not have room enough for it." (Malachi 3:7–10)

This is the only place in the Bible where the Lord challenges us to test
Him, and the challenge is with strong words. If we give less than ten
percent, we will be cursed, and if we give ten percent, we will be
blessed a great deal. Therefore, tithing is one of the smartest things we
can do, and not tithing is one of the dumbest things we can do.

Consider the following fictitious story: A man had an appointment
for counseling with his pastor at his church. The pastor was not there,
and while waiting in the lobby, he noticed a safe behind the door to
another room. Being curious, he walked toward it and found the words
"God's Money" written at the top of the safe. He wondered if it contained the Sunday offerings, and his curiosity led him to pull on the
door handle. To his surprise, the safe door opened, and inside on the
top shelf was a random pile of cash. There were ones, fives, tens, twen-
ties, fifties, and even a few hundreds. It clearly totaled in the thousands.

He quickly shut the door before anyone saw him and sat back down
in the lobby. After a moment of thinking about his money problems,
he had a fleeting thought of taking some cash from the safe, but then
said to himself that he absolutely can't, that it would be horrible to steal
God's money, and worse, God would know.

He then got a call on his cell phone from the pastor, stating that he
would arrive in about five minutes, and apologizing for no one being
there, explaining that his secretary was out sick that day. The man began going over in his mind all the bills he had to pay, and began feeling
the heaviness of worry. He thought, "new-found cash would surely ease

my worry, this big church will not miss what I take anyway, and surely God will forgive me because of my predicament." The man walked to the safe, looked around to make sure no one was in sight, and quickly opened it and grabbed a fistful of money and stuffed it in his pocket. He hurriedly walked back to his chair to wait on the pastor to arrive.

How bad was this man? He just robbed God! God declared in Malachi 3:8–9 that when we don't give our tithes and offerings, we rob Him. What is the difference? You might say, "But this man robbed money that others chose to give to God." That is correct, and at the moment others tithed, it was in God's possession. But anytime the man receives a paycheck and puts money in his wallet or checkbook, ten percent is God's money. It was never the man's money, he simply had possession of it. Not putting it in "God's Money" safe is no different than taking money *from* "God's Money" safe.

The man was tested, and he failed.

As we are paid, do we pass the test? Why don't we turn the test around on God. Say, "Okay, God, you know I can't afford to tithe, but you said 'test me on this,' and so I am passing your test and handing over your ten percent, so now the test is on you." Is that being a smart aleck? Absolutely not! God said to test Him. He wants us to test Him.

By my own experiences, and by what I have been told about financial blessings received by others who gave ten percent or more, I am convinced that the good Lord will not allow us to outgive Him. In fact, Jesus promised: *"Give, and it will be given to you. A good measure, pressed down, shaken together and running over, will be poured into your lap. For with the measure you use, it will be measured to you"* (Luke 6:38). The following also supports this truth: *"One man gives freely, yet gains even more; another withholds unduly, but comes to poverty"* (Proverbs 11:24). The apostle Paul supports it as well: *Whoever sows sparingly will also reap sparingly, and whoever sows generously will also reap generously"* (2 Corinthians 9:6). We are also promised a blessing if we give of our firstfruits: *"Honor the Lord with your wealth, with the firstfruits of all your crops; then your barns will be filled to overflowing, and your vats will brim over with new wine"* (Proverbs 3:9–10).

I know of a church in Nashville that offers a 90-day guarantee. It promises that anyone who is not sufficiently blessed after committing to tithe during that 90-day period will have their money returned. It is a church with thousands of members. The pastor told me that all who have sought a refund after 90 days turned out to have not actually tithed ten percent.

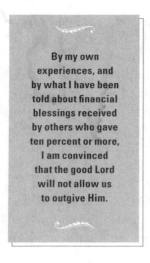

By my own experiences, and by what I have been told about financial blessings received by others who gave ten percent or more, I am convinced that the good Lord will not allow us to outgive Him.

For years, I struggled with paying my bills as they came due, oftentimes having to borrow money to do so. Sometimes, although rarely, I fell back on my tithing. I did not feel good about that at all, and many times, I would just "grit my teeth" and write a check for ten percent of my income for the month, forcing myself not to look at my checkbook to verify whether I would be able to make it to the next pay period; I called it "blind giving." As 2 Corinthians 4:7 says, *"We live by faith, not by sight."* Looking back, I cannot think of a time when I exercised "blind giving" that I wasn't blessed financially within one to four weeks. I was always amazed at how God always protected me. Instead of tithing setting me back financially, it put me ahead, which is one of my favorite examples of the precepts of Christianity that seem mysteriously antithetical.

I cannot leave this subject without interjecting a bit of common sense. We should not think that tithing will make up for irresponsible living. We should do all we can to make ends meet, give ten percent to God, and He will take it from there.

Worship the Lord Your God

"Worship the Lord your God, and serve him only" (Matthew 4:10). Jesus explains that *"true worshipers will worship the Father in spirit and truth, for they are the kind of worshipers the Father seeks. God is spirit, and his worshipers must worship in spirit and in truth"* (John 4:23–24; emphasis added).

The apostle Paul said that, in view of God's mercy, our spiritual act of worship is to offer our bodies as a living sacrifice, holy and pleasing to God (Romans 12:1). It could very well be that God views our highest form of worship as offering ourselves in full surrender to His will. Interestingly, Rebecca Springer states in her book *Within Heaven's Gates* that, while in heaven, her niece, Mae, said that our best worship is to do His blessed will (Springer, 38).

What other ways are considered worshiping in spirit? No particular manner of worship is called for in the New Testament other than to *"worship God acceptably with reverence and awe, for our 'God is a consuming fire'"* (Hebrews 12:28–29). The apostle Paul finds it acceptable to lift our hands in prayer: *"I want men everywhere to lift up holy hands in prayer, without anger or disputing"* (1 Timothy 2:8). Although external regulations of worship in the old order no longer apply (Hebrews 9:1), I found no prohibition in the New Testament of the ways of worship of the Old Testament.

In the Old Testament, Nehemiah stated that people worshiped by raising their hands, speaking in unison, and bowing down with their faces to the ground (Nehemiah 8:6). The Psalms have more to say about our manner of worship:

- *"Come, let us bow down in worship, let us kneel before the LORD our Maker"* (Psalm 95:6).
- *"Let them praise his name with dancing and make music to him with tambourine and harp. For the LORD takes delight in his people"* (Psalm 149:3–4).
- *"Shout for joy to the LORD, all the earth. Worship the LORD with gladness; come before him with joyful songs"* (Psalm 100:1–2).
- *"Lift up your hands in the sanctuary and praise the LORD"* (Psalm 134:2).
- *"Praise him with the sounding of the trumpet, praise him with the harp and lyre, praise him with tambourine and dancing, praise him with the strings and flute, praise him with the clash of cymbals, praise him with resounding cymbals"* (Psalm 150:3–5).

It appears that none of the above is mandatory—it's merely acceptable. Is it acceptable to worship in a reserved and quiet manner or without musical instruments? I found no place in the Bible where this is addressed. Because the Bible provides no instruction on how to worship, it appears that all ways are acceptable so long as we worship under the general instruction to do so in spirit and in truth and with reverence and awe.

If we're moving to the music and lifting our arms high in the air without an engagement of our hearts, what good is it, for Jesus said that if our hearts are far from Him during worship, we are worshiping in vain (Matthew 15:8–9). If we worship in stillness but our hearts are filled with passion, how can that not be pleasing to God? Based on Scripture, although the Lord delights in our praising Him with music and dancing during worship, His heart is moved mostly by the level of engagement of ours.

Worshiping in spirit does not concern frequency, for I found no Scripture that imposes an obligation in that regard other than to keep the seventh day of the week holy. Some might consider that to mean we are to attend church each week, but that is not expressly stated. Although it is certainly good to attend church every week (there is debate among denominations as to whether Saturday or Sunday is the appropriate day), we should be careful not to fall into a false sense of security in believing, however slightly, that doing so somehow serves as a substitute for demonstrating our love through deeds, that we have done our duty or "served our time" for the week. It is so easy to fall into that mindset. As demonstrated earlier in this book, not serving others and otherwise not obeying God is a sin. We can do things to cover over a multitude of sins (see chapter 10), but nothing in Scripture says that a certain amount of time in worship covers sins.

What about the command of Jesus in John 4:24 to worship in truth? After all, zealous worship is of no avail if it is without knowledge (Romans 10:1–4). Being taught by those who ignore some Scripture or water it down by not relaying the fullness of God's expectations only blinds us to the ways in which the Lord expects us to obey Him, and *"if a blind man leads a blind man, both will fall into a pit"* (Matthew 15:14). Will God actually allow heaven to escape us by merely being taught in the wrong way? Yes! This is a reason why Jesus had such strong words of condemnation for the Pharisees, the religious teachers of His day: *"Woe*

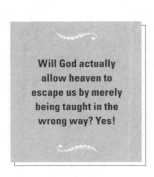

Will God actually allow heaven to escape us by merely being taught in the wrong way? Yes!

to you experts in the law, because you have taken away the key to knowledge. You yourselves have not entered, and you have hindered those who were entering" (Luke 11:52). A wrong messenger can shut the kingdom of heaven in our faces. *"Woe to you, teachers of the law and Pharisees, you hypocrites! You shut the kingdom of heaven in men's faces. You yourselves do not enter, nor will you let those enter who are trying to. Woe to you, teachers of the law and Pharisees, you hypocrites! You travel over land and sea to win a single convert, and when he becomes one, you make him twice as much a son of hell as you are"* (Matthew 23:13–15). The wrong messenger can make us sons of hell! Wow, those are strong words. There is no doubt that Jesus is very serious about correct teachings!

As we have seen, we are to *"make every effort to enter through the narrow door, because many, I tell you, will try to enter and will not be able to"* (Luke 13:24). What good is it to make every effort if they are done in blindness to what effort is required? The house of truth that we are attempting to build, within which we stand firm against the torrential winds of temptation and greed, is of little value if it crumbles under the unknowing instability of the soil of poor instruction on which it lies. Therefore, we must verify everything we are taught by going to the Word and earnestly seeking its true meaning, for a misinterpretation can lead to our own destruction. As the apostle Peter said in reference to the biblical letters of Paul: *"His letters contain some things that are hard to understand, which ignorant and unstable people distort, as they do the other Scriptures, to their own destruction"* (2 Peter 3:16).

I'm reminded of when I was a child on a baseball team. During batting practice, my coach always threw the ball more slowly than it was thrown in the game. I hit well at practice, but at the games, I consistently hit pop-ups. My coach did me no favors by "watering down" the game in practice. Similarly, our ministers do us no favors by "watering down" Scripture or ignoring uncomfortable parts. I want pitches thrown at me as hard and fast as those delivered by Jesus. Hitting slow pitches well at practice made me feel good. But during the game, when it counted, I felt terrible; with fast pitches, I couldn't even get on base.

In the game of life, I want to get on base, to get in the game and find the gate that leads to eternal life, where my citizenship awaits me (Philippians 3:20). I want to embrace the reality of the difficulty of the pitches that God throws at me. I want to take a swing at the ball of truth, and with practice, get better and better, and never give up on my efforts to improve my game. Then, I can bask in the peace and joy of knowing that all my practices were worthwhile, that they prepared me for the game of life. From the truth, I want nothing watered down and nothing taken away.

That is my mission with this book. I'm driven to reveal the truth, the whole truth, and nothing but the truth on the subject of what it takes to go to heaven so that all who read this book come to know what they need to know, not what they want to know. Those who teach to please men are not servants of Christ (Galatians 1:10). We get enough feel-good messages that appear to be geared more toward conveying what people want to hear than toward taking on the risk of making them uncomfortable with the truth. If this book makes you feel good,

that's great. If it makes you feel convicted, that is not its purpose; however, if feeling convicted motivates you to do what it takes to go to
heaven, then it has served its purpose.

Are we required to pray to go to heaven? In Matthew 6:5–13, Jesus
instructed us on how we should pray, which is the Lord's Prayer. Because His instruction appears to be advice as opposed to a command,
the Lord's Prayer is not included in this chapter. This chapter includes
only the commands of God, as spoken through Jesus and the apostles.
However, calling on the assistance of the Lord through prayer is essential in enabling us to live according to the
Spirit. In other words, praying is not an end in
and of itself to go to heaven, but it is a means
to an end, and therefore it is critical. It stands
to reason that we should *pray in the Spirit on
all occasions with all kinds of prayers and requests*
(Ephesians 6:18; see Colossians 4:2).

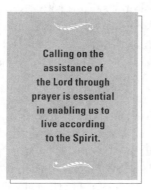

Calling on the
assistance of
the Lord through
prayer is essential
in enabling us to
live according
to the Spirit.

Prayer also has the additional benefit
of bringing peace of mind over us. *"Do not
be anxious about anything, but in everything, by
prayer and petition, with thanksgiving, present your
requests to God. And the peace of God, which transcends all understanding, will
guard your hearts and your minds in Christ Jesus"* (Philippians 4:6–7).

Lead Others to Christ

One of the most noted commands of Jesus is His final one, given to
His eleven disciples before He ascended to heaven: *"All authority in
heaven and on earth has been given to me. Therefore go and make disciples of
all nations, baptizing them in the name of the Father and of the Son and of the
Holy Spirit, and* teaching them to obey everything I have commanded
you. *And surely I am with you always, to the very end of the age"* (Matthew
28:18–20; emphasis added). I can think of not a greater feeling than
that which would come from Jesus walking up to me in heaven and
pointing to a friend across the way and saying, "See your friend Robert
over there? If it weren't for you, he wouldn't be here." When that happens, I'll be grinning wide as I run to Robert to give him a high five!
We all should do what it takes to usher others into heaven so that we
can celebrate with them upon arriving there.

Bringing others to Christ should involve more than informing them of His love and stating that if they accept Him as their Savior, they will be saved, for if they don't repent, their salvation will be lost. Therefore, it is critical that we expose them to the teachings of Jesus and encourage them to live a Christian life. As stated in Matthew 28:18–20, Jesus charged His disciples to teach others to obey everything He commanded. Obviously, we must learn His commands before we can teach them. Giving them a copy of this book is a good start, but all of us also need one-on-one training: *"Let the word of Christ dwell in you richly as you teach and admonish one another with all wisdom"* (Colossians 3:16). In fact, we should learn more of Scripture than just the commands of Jesus, for *"all Scripture is God-breathed and is useful for teaching, rebuking, correcting and training in righteousness, so that the man of God may be thoroughly equipped for every good work"* (2 Timothy 3:16–17; see also 2 Samuel 22:31; John 14:24; 1 Corinthians 1:17; 1 Peter 1:25; 2 Peter 1:20–21).

In 2 Timothy 4:2, the apostle Paul instructed Timothy to preach the Word and *"rebuke and encourage—with great patience and careful instruction."* To encourage others, *"let us consider how we may spur one another on toward love and good deeds"* (Hebrews 10:24). Encouragement also helps people escape the threat of developing a hardened heart that justifies sin: *"Encourage one another daily, as long as it is called today, so that none of you may be hardened by sin's deceitfulness"* (Hebrews 3:13). As to the instruction to rebuke, it is much easier to flatter, but withholding a proper rebuke is not the Lord's will: *"He who rebukes a man will in the end gain more favor than he who has a flattering tongue"* (Proverbs 28:23). This earth is our school for learning obedience; we learn more through rebuke than flattery. The wise welcome it: *"Do not rebuke a mocker or he will hate you; rebuke a wise man and he will love you"* (Proverbs 9:8).

> This earth is our school for learning obedience; we learn more through rebuke than flattery. The wise welcome it.

We are to help each other stay in alignment with the Lord's commands: *"It was he who gave some to be apostles, some to be prophets, some to be evangelists, and some to be pastors and teachers, to prepare God's people for works of service, so that the body of Christ may be built up until we all reach unity in the faith and in the knowledge of the Son of God and become mature, attaining to the whole measure of the fullness of Christ"* (Ephesians 4:11–13). In the end, *"we proclaim him, admonishing and teaching everyone with all wisdom, so that we may present everyone perfect in Christ"* (Colossians 1:28).

One of the best ways to encourage others to live in Christian ways is by example: *"Let your light shine before men, that they may see your good deeds and praise your Father in heaven"* (Matthew 5:16). I love the following story: There was a soldier who was wounded in battle. The padre crept out and did what he could for him. He stayed with him when the remainder of the troops retreated. In the heat of the day, he gave him water from his own water bottle, while he himself remained parched with thirst. In the night, when the frost came down, he covered the wounded man with his own coat, and finally wrapped him up in even more of his clothes to save him from the cold. In the end, the wounded man looked up at the padre. "Padre," he said, "you're a Christian?" "I try to be," said the padre. "Then," said the wounded man, "if Christianity makes a man do for another man what you have done for me, tell me about it, because I want it."

So proud the Lord must be when we represent Christianity like that. If we carry the badge of Christianity, we should honor Jesus by modeling a Christian lifestyle, drawing people in by being the kind of person others would like to be. If we expose the attributes of Christianity by example, our effectiveness at bringing others to Christ will be enhanced. Those who observe Christians as examples to follow in their own efforts to improve themselves should not consider them hypocrites for not being perfect. We all sin, and our striving to improve is a journey that never ends. None of us ever becomes a faultless model Christian to mimic, and don't be discouraged if you see a Christian do something that is unChristian-like. We should all simply teach and admonish each other in our never-ending journey to improve ourselves.

We should also guard ourselves from thinking that the unsaved are "objects" for opportunity to place another mark on the chalkboard of "the saved." They are people. We bring others to Christianity because we genuinely care about them, not to keep score in the game of Christian achievement. We *"are a mist that appears for a little while and then vanishes"* (James 4:14). During our short time, the two most fundamental reasons for being here are these: First, we are to make every effort to enter through the narrow door to make our hope for salvation sure; second, we are to teach and encourage others to make every effort to enter through the narrow door to make *their* hope for salvation sure. We should be careful not to lose that perspective: This earth is, above all, our school to train us to be godly and prepare us for works of service (Ephesians 4:12). It is not the real life—the real life is heaven.

I've had a few friends put this book down without reading much of it, feeling defeated, believing they cannot carry out all that God expects or simply not willing to do so. It breaks my heart: First, though God's expectations appear daunting, upon being transformed in the way we think, they're not, for when we are transformed, we overcome the world, which makes God's commands not burdensome (1 John 5:3–4; see Matthew 11:30). Second, living by God's ways is the key to true joy, a joy that is rich and real. Third, based on the following Scripture, if we knew what heaven was like, we would be willing to "sacrifice" *all* we have here in order to go there, and we would do it with *joy*: *"The kingdom of heaven is like treasure hidden in a field. When a man found it, he hid it again, and then in his joy went and sold all he had and bought that field. Again, the kingdom of heaven is like a merchant looking for fine pearls. When he found one of great value, he went away and sold everything he had and bought it"* (Matthew 13:44–46). Soak in this Scripture. Believe it! Then you will be more open to being transformed to a new way of thinking, as explained in the next chapter, so that the "burden" of sacrifice no longer seems like a burden.

Do Not Be Bound by Man-Made Rules

We should be careful not to be bound by man-made rules that are not supported by Scripture. The apostle Paul said, *"Since you died with Christ to the basic principles of this world, why, as though you still belonged to it, do you submit to its rules: 'Do not handle! Do not taste! Do not touch!'? These are all destined to perish with use, because they are based on human commands and teachings. Such regulations indeed have an appearance of wisdom, with their self-imposed worship, their false humility and their harsh treatment of the body, but they lack any value in restraining sensual indulgence"* (Colossians 2:20–22; emphasis added).

Not only is obeying man-made rules done in vain, but because those efforts might give us a false sense of having done enough for the Lord, we might do less in fulfilling His true will. Worse, some can be counterproductive, for many who were raised under strict man-made "religious" rules turn away from Christianity later in life because of them. God warned us from about 1400 B.C., when Deuteronomy was written, not to add to His commands or subtract from them: *"Do not*

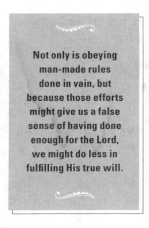

Not only is obeying man-made rules done in vain, but because those efforts might give us a false sense of having done enough for the Lord, we might do less in fulfilling His true will.

add to what I command you and do not subtract from it, but keep the commands of the LORD your God that I give you" (Deuteronomy 4:2).

Man-made teachings can also result in our worshiping "in vain": *"These people honor me with their lips, but their hearts are far from me. They worship me in vain; their teachings are but rules taught by men"* (Matthew 15:8–9).

To the Pharisees, the experts in man-made religious law, Jesus spoke these harsh words: *"You experts in the law, woe to you, because you load people down with burdens they can hardly carry, and you yourselves will not lift one finger to help them"* (Luke 11:46). This tells us that we are not to interpret the law in a way that imposes unnecessary burdens on us, but what matters is living our lives in love, which certainly includes helping others.

A lady once told me that the waitresses at the restaurant where she works try to avoid working the Sunday lunch shift because of the low-tipping church crowd. That makes me sick! Do many of us Christians get wrapped up in rule-compliance such as weekly church attendance, but miss the paramount message that we are to do unto others as we would have them do unto us? We Christians carry the badge of Christianity, and we should never embarrass God by being stingy givers.

I used to go to church every Sunday under a sense of duty. I didn't like going sometimes, but felt good when I went, knowing that I had "served my time" for the week. In between Sundays, I gave very little thought to ways in which I could help others. Now, I go to church for nourishment and to worship the Lord, and I realize that I produce fruit by helping others, not by "serving my time" in church.

The church crowd that has lunch at my friend's restaurant should look for ways to produce fruit, such as tipping well, so that their light shines before men, that others will see their good deeds and praise our Father in heaven (Matthew 5:16). Those who can't afford to tip well should consider ordering a vegetable plate instead of a meat and three, and add the difference to the tip. Whether in big sacrifices or small, we should always look for ways to be generous. It is so easy to fall into rule-compliance and find that our hearts have drifted away. We are to continually train ourselves to be godly (1 Timothy 4:7), mostly by focusing on loving. We begin by being transformed to a new way of thinking.

~ 9 ~

Must We Be Transformed to a New Way of Thinking?

Doing all that God asks of us can seem daunting. For the most part, He calls us to do the following: God wants us to love Him with all our heart, soul, mind, and strength, and to love our neighbor as ourselves (Luke 10:27); we are to discontinue being self-seeking (Romans 2:8), consider others better than ourselves (Philippians 2:3), no longer seek our own good but the good of others (1 Corinthians 10:24), no longer live for ourselves (2 Corinthians 5:15), share our material possessions with our brothers in need (1 John 3:17), including our tunics and our food (Luke 3:11), carry each other's burdens (Galatians 6:2), be devoted to one another in brotherly love (Romans 12:10), love each other as brothers (Hebrews 13:1), and carry out other acts of selflessness. We are to do these things for all, including the less fortunate (Matthew 25:45), the weak (Romans 15:1; 1 Thessalonians 5:14), and the orphans and widows (James 1:27); we are to entertain strangers and remember those who are mistreated as though we ourselves were suffering (Hebrews 13:2–3); we are to love our enemies (Matthew 5:44; Luke 6:27, 35), including feeding them and giving them something to drink (Romans 12:17–21); and we are to be proactive in pursuing these things (Matthew 25:14–30; Luke 17:7–10; James 4:17). Overall, we are to *make every effort to enter through the narrow door, because many, I tell you, will try to enter and will not be able to*" (Luke 13:24).

Whew, that's a lot! We have two ways to approach what appears to be a very heavy load:

1. We can force ourselves to comply with the above without addressing the conflicting draw of our selfish nature; or
2. We can adopt a new way of thinking, with love as its foundation, that subverts our selfish nature and raises up a nature of selflessness so that we *want* to give more—and we expect less for ourselves.

Obviously, the second approach is better, and when the transition penetrates your core, these worldly "burdens" feel lighter and giving seems to be less of a sacrifice, if at all, for your thoughts will become less about yourself and more about others. In essence, we train ourselves to get out of ourselves and into the hearts of others, and our actions follow those thoughts.

We Are to Be Born Again

Getting out of ourselves and into the hearts of others needs to reach to the core of us. We are to be transformed to a new person as though we are born again. Jesus said that unless we change to that extent, we will not see heaven: *"I tell you the truth, no one can see the kingdom of God unless he is born again"* (John 3:3). (The kingdom of God is heaven [Matthew 19:22–26; Mark 9:47; Luke 13:23–30] and it can be within us [Luke 11:20–26; 17:20–21]). In this Scripture, Jesus was referring to heaven. Jesus said that few *find* the small gate to heaven (Matthew 7:21). Could it be because few know or believe that we must be born again?

Perhaps some of us can do the will of God without being born again, but it's more difficult that way (see 1 John 5:3–4), and will it last? That will be addressed later in this chapter, as well as learning *how* we are born again. But first, let's examine Scripture as to what "born again" means.

What Does "Born Again" Mean?

No place in the New Testament is the phrase "born again" clearly defined, but we can garner a significant indication of what it means by synthesizing Scriptures.

After the statement from Jesus in John 3:3 that no one can see the kingdom of God unless he is born again, Nicodemus asked what He meant by that. Jesus said that it is being born of water and the Spirit, that flesh gives birth to flesh, but the Spirit gives birth to spirit; He said that the wind blows wherever it pleases and you hear its sounds, but you cannot tell where it comes from or where it is going, and so it is with everyone born of the Spirit (John 3:5–8). This tells us that, by some mysterious way, the Holy Spirit gives birth to the spirit within us; but we need the assistance of additional Scripture to understand the breadth of what "born again" means and to understand the type of change that comes over us to indicate that we have been born again.

James said that God chose to give us birth through the word of truth (James 1:18). Consistently, Peter said that we are born again through the Word of God: *"Now that you have purified yourselves by obeying the truth so that you have sincere love for your brothers, love one another deeply, from the heart. For you have been born again, not of perishable seed, but of imperishable, through the living and enduring word of God"* (1 Peter 1:22–23). This Scripture tells us that when we are "born again," we obey the truth, which brings us to have sincere love for our brothers. John said in 1 John 2:29 that everyone who does what is right has been born of Him (Jesus). Because obeying the truth and doing what is right are the same thing, and one is from being born again and the other is from being born of Him, then being born again is the same as being born of Him. One of the Greek definitions for "again" is "from above," and thus, "born again" can mean "born from above."* By being born "of Him" or born "from above," we can surmise that being born again means we become more godly, which is consistent with our call to be *"transformed into his [God's] likeness"* (2 Corinthians 3:18).

The following supports that explanation: *"Yet to all who received him [Jesus], to those who believed in his name, he gave the right to become children of God—children born not of natural descent, nor of human decision or a husband's will, but born of God"* (John 1:12–13). This Scripture states that receiving Jesus gives us the right to be born of God, which means it is not a certainty. We exercise that right by choosing to begin a process of being born of God, which, as stated above, is the same as being born again, to be transformed into His likeness.

The following Scriptures from the apostle Paul tell us that we are to become a new person:

---

* Goodrick and Kohlenberger, *Strongest NIV Exhaustive Concordance,* s.v. "again."

- *"You have taken off your old self with its practices and have put on the new self"* (Colossians 3:9–10).
- *"You were taught, with regard to your former way of life, to put off your old self, which is being corrupted by its deceitful desires; to be made new in the attitude of your minds; and to put on the new self, created to be like God in true righteousness and holiness"* (Ephesians 4:22–24).
- *Neither circumcision nor uncircumcision means anything; what counts is a new creation"* (Galatians 6:15). (The custom taught by Moses was that only the circumcised can be saved [Acts 15:1].)
- *"Put to death, therefore, whatever belongs to your earthy nature: . . . Because of these, the wrath of God is coming"* (Colossians 3:5–6).
- *"If anyone is in Christ, he is a new creation; the old has gone, the new has come!"* (2 Corinthians 5:17; see also 2 Corinthians 3:7–8).

Collectively, these verses say that we are to put off our old self, our earthly nature, and become a new creation, with a new attitude, to "be like God in true righteousness and holiness." Because that is consistent with the previously stated summation that being born again means we become more godly, being born again means we are to become a new creation.

It makes sense that to be born again, we die first. After death, we rethink everything; we begin again at the beginning— like a child.

To what extent are we to become a new creation? We begin by *crucifying* and *burying* our old ways: *"For we know that our old self was crucified with him so that the body of sin might be done away with . . ."* (Romans 6:6). *"Don't you know that all of us who were baptized into Christ Jesus were baptized into his death? We were therefore buried with him through baptism into death in order that, just as Christ was raised from the dead through the glory of the Father, we too may live a new life"* (Romans 6:2–4). It makes sense that to be born again, we die first. After death, we rethink everything; we begin again at the beginning—like a child.

Why Need We Be Born Again to Obey?

Jesus said we will not see the kingdom of God (heaven) without being born again (John 3:3). That is reason enough for why we need to be born again. For those who would like to know *why* we cannot see heaven without being born again, I offer the following: We learned in chapter 5 that we must do the will of the Father to go to heaven. Must we be "born again" to obey? Can't we simply obey? Frankly, I do not think any of us can stay the course of meeting God's high standards without fully transforming how we think. We might do well for a week, a month, or a few years, but for a lifetime?

Obedience that stands the test of time comes from an outflow of love that is cultivated through knowledge of the Word, putting the Word into practice, and the assistance of the sanctifying work of Holy Spirit (see Philippians 2:13; 2 Thessalonians 2:13; 1 Peter 1:2) so that, with time, the love in us overcomes our sinful, selfish nature. We are born again as new creations, with a new core of how we think, and from that core will flow no more sin, except for occasional deviations. We can choose to avoid the conversion process—being born again—and instead, simply put our best foot forward with a determination to obey. But in the end, what we do and don't do flows from the core of us—our earthly self-seeking, sinful nature—and we will slip into our old ways.

> We can choose to avoid the conversion process—being born again—and instead, simply put our best foot forward with a determination to obey. But in the end, what we do and don't do flows from the core of us—our earthly self-seeking, sinful nature—and we will slip into our old ways.

How to Be Born Again—Changes in Perception

Without being born again, the burden of God's expectations of carrying out what God expects as reflected in the first page of this chapter (which, in a nutshell, is to give to others) is simply too heavy. To lighten the "burden," we need to overhaul how we think. The Bible teaches us to think as follows, which I believe is the best line of thinking to lighten the burden: "It's not about me, I truly care about others, and I can't outgive the Lord, anyway."

1. Being Born Again, We Remove the Perception That Giving Is a Sacrifice

This section addresses the part "I can't outgive the Lord, anyway." When we understand that and truly believe it, how can we think that giving is sacrifice? (The following tell us that we cannot outgive the Lord: Deuteronomy 15:10; Proverbs 3:9–10, 11:24, 19:17; Ecclesiastes 11:1–2; Malachi 3:8–10; Mark 4:24–25; Luke 6:38; and 2 Corinthians 9:6–11.)

The Christian life requires us to shift our focus from living mainly for ourselves to living a life of helping and giving. When we give, we receive joy. God wired us that way. No training or rethinking is required—it simply comes to us. It's been referred to as "helper's high." The problem is this: When we give, we perceive it as a sacrifice. Thus, a decision to give involves weighing the perceived sacrifices we make by giving against the joy of giving. Conversion tips the scales by removing the perception that giving is a sacrifice, thus removing the "weight" of giving. With weight removed from that side of the scales, but the joy of giving remaining on the other side, the joy side is received without interference.

To help illustrate, think of how much fun would it be to give away other people's possessions and money. We would feel the fullness of the joy of giving without any interference because it would be without sacrifice on our part. For example, a new convenience store called Twice Daily opened up recently a block away from my office. In the first few weeks, they gave away free coffee and drinks, apparently to lure people into the store and get them in the habit of coming in twice daily. The joy of giving is very evident in the employees as they announce with excitement, "Free drinks and coffee!" They feel the joy of giving without interference—they're not paying for it. Because conversion removes the perception that giving is a sacrifice, we can receive the same joy of giving *our* possessions and money as the people at Twice Daily receive when giving *others'* possessions and money. Okay, perhaps it isn't *exactly* the same, but it should be close, actually, very close.

When we are born again by a renewing of our minds in that way, the "burden" of serving God is lifted and our joy that comes naturally from giving elevates. By that explanation, we have a deeper understanding of the following Scriptures:

- *"For my yoke is easy and my burden is light"* (Matthew 11:30).
- *"If you obey my commands, you will remain in my love, just as I have obeyed my Father's commands and remain in his love. I have told you this so that my joy may be in you and that your joy may be complete"* (John 15:10–11).

- *"And his commands are not burdensome, for everyone born of God over-comes the world"* (1 John 5:3–4).

2. Being Born Again, We Find More Joy in Giving

The emphasis in the last section was on the part "I can't outgive the Lord anyway." In this section, the emphasis is on the part "It's not about me, and I truly care about others."

Let's begin with a clarification. Learning that "it's not about me" does not mean that we go so far as to become martyrs; we can still do for ourselves, we just simply also do to others as we would have them do to us (Luke 6:27–31). And we can keep for ourselves a reasonable amount of wealth and possessions so long as we are rich toward God* (Luke 12:16–21), are not eager to get rich (Proverbs 28:20), are not trying to feed our selfish ambitions (Galatians 5:19–25; see Philippians 2:3–4), are not putting our hope in money (1 Timothy 6:17–19), are not boasting in money (1 John 2:15–17), and are not serving money (we cannot serve both God and money [Matthew 6:24]).

We learned in 1 John 5:3–4 that *"his commands are not burdensome, for everyone born of God overcomes the world."* Broken down, this states that when we are born of God, we overcome the world, and when we overcome the world, God's commands are not burdensome. I believe the world that we are to overcome is its passions and desires that are fueled by "it's about me" way of thinking. Therefore, when we are *born of God*, which requires a full commitment, it gets us out of the "it's about me" way of thinking, and God's commands are not burdensome.

The question that comes to mind is this: The first step—fully committing—requires a great deal of effort. How do we make something that requires a great deal of effort end up not being burdensome? The answer is in how we view it.

---

* Not only is it acceptable to God to have a reasonable amount of wealth and possessions when we are rich toward Him, but He will reward us financially when we are: *"Now he [God] who supplies seed to the sower and bread for food will also supply and increase your store of seed and will enlarge the harvest of your righteousness. You will be made rich in every way so that you can be generous on every occasion, and through us your generosity will result in thanksgiving to God"* (2 Corinthians 9:10–11). There is a caveat regarding money: We must be very careful on matters related to it, for it is deceptive (Matthew 13:22), and *"some people, eager for money, have wandered from the faith and pierced themselves with many griefs"* (1 Timothy 6:10).

For example, my brother-in-law loves to race his Porsche on the racetrack, which requires a great deal of effort. He has to get his car race-ready, which requires different wheels, tires, seats, steering wheel, suspension, refinements of the car body for reduced wind resistance and increased downforce, and adjustments of the engine. On race day, he has to hook up a trailer to his truck, set up ramps to the trailer to drive his race car on, strap down the car on the trailer, put cabinets of tools and a jack and other items in the bed of his truck, and drive for hours to the racetrack. When there, he must unload everything into the pit garage, check various items regarding the car, put on his fireproof race suit and helmet, and then begin racing. After racing two to four hours, he has to go through the whole process again, but in reverse.

For me, it would be entirely too much effort and expense for the return, and thus, I would find all those tasks very burdensome. For my brother-in-law, he loves every minute of every part of the process because he loves to race. No part of it is burdensome to him. In the same way, fulfilling God's expectations to give to others is not considered burdensome by those who find great joy in it.

Previously, I stated that God wired us to receive joy in giving—it just comes to us. We can increase that joy by getting out of the "it's about me" way of thinking and really caring about others. When adding that increase in joy in giving to our already being wired to receive joy in giving, the joy is elevated to a level that makes the expense and efforts of giving, even in a big way, not seem burdensome.

You might ask why the fullness of the joy of giving applies only to those who fully commit to obeying God as opposed to those who merely take a stab at it. We know that giving brings joy. That joy leads to more giving, which in turn leads to more joy, which in turn, leads to more giving—they feed off each other. Second, until we fully commit, I don't believe we will be fully transformed to think that "It's not about me, I truly care about others, and I can't outgive the Lord, anyway." Those who commit in part, who merely take a stab at a Christian walk, will not think that way, at least not fully.

In conclusion of all this, there is less burden for those who fully commit to following God's ways than for those who take a stab at it. That is one of the greatest mysteries and ironies of Christianity until we break it down logically this way. A more important conclusion is this: When the yoke of Jesus is easy, the burden is light, and joy is given us, we are much more likely to stay the course of obeying God. That is what happens to the born again, and I believe that is why Jesus told us that only the born again go to heaven.

Why Need We Be Born Again to Go to Heaven?

As stated before, for God's perfect will to be done in heaven, only those committed to obey may go there. If we bypassed a conversion to a born-again state, reshaped in how we think, and somehow were able to sweat out our deeds that we feel are necessary to enter heaven, checking them off as we go in anticipation of taking a sigh of relief upon reaching the finish line at the pearly gates, what will be our motivation to continue a life of obedience toward God upon arriving there? Will we "run out of gas" upon reaching the finish line? Will we be tired and weary and thankful that we finally made it—and then remove the yoke of our checklist of tasks in anticipation of reaping our reward? If that is our mindset upon reaching heaven, what good are we there to God? Will He have control of us so that His will can be done there, as stated in the Lord's Prayer? Will God ignore His warnings that we are to be converted to a new way of thinking here, and there, instantly and supernaturally, convert us? Nothing in the Bible indicates that will happen.

That is why we are not to think that we can earn our way to heaven, because a person who thinks he earns his way and thus bypasses being converted is a person who is of little value upon arriving there. Here, we are to develop a nature of giving and obedience, doing deeds not for something in return, but because we simply want to—it's who we have become. A heaven that includes only those whose nature has been converted in that way is a heaven of God's followers whom God can depend on to do His will.

The apostle Paul made the following statement to make it clear that we are not to pursue entrance to heaven through earning it: *"For it is by grace you have been saved, through faith— and this not from yourselves, it is the gift of God— not by works, so that no one can boast"* (Ephesians

> **We are not to think that we can earn our way to heaven, because a person who thinks he earns his way and thus bypasses being converted is a person who is of little value upon arriving there.**

2:8–9). As to Jesus telling us to make every effort to enter through the narrow door (Luke 13:24), it is the effort to become a different person, centered on love, on which we are to focus (2 Peter 1:5–7),* not necessarily on making every effort to do works. If, however, we have sufficiently become a different person, we will do good works. After all, we are *"created in Christ Jesus to do good works"* (Ephesians 2:10), and in fact, we are to be *"eager to do what is good"* (Titus 2:14). In summary, proof of being a Christian is in the pudding.

Here's an example. A preacher told me that a Christian asked him if it is a sin to resent having to take care of her aging parents. The resentment itself is not a sin. That person should examine herself, however, to determine if she has been reborn by a sufficient renewal of her mind. If she hasn't, that is a contributing factor in her resentment, and worse, she will not see the kingdom of God (heaven). If she has been reborn, she probably will not resent caring for her parents. Notice that I said "probably," for it depends on the entire situation. But one who is reborn to a new way of thinking will find the efforts to be much less burdensome, if at all, because the love for God, all humans, and especially one's parents, will elevate the joy on one side of the scales, and minimize the perceived sacrifice on the other side.

Anyone who doubts whether we are to stay the course of loving and obeying after entering heaven should know this—even that is not good enough to the extent we understand here what it means to love and obey: We are to rise to an even higher level upon arriving in heaven. Jesus said: *"I tell you the truth: Among those born of women there has not risen anyone greater than John the Baptist; yet he who is least in the kingdom of heaven is greater than he"* (Matthew 11:11). Therefore, even the greatest here are not at heaven's level of greatness, but must rise to that level. Jesus warned us that even saying "you fool" puts us in danger of not going to heaven (Matthew 5:22), which tells us that the standards there are very high.

Here, we're taught the concept of brotherhood—the expectation that we love others as ourselves, that my needs are no more important than my brother's needs, and vice versa. It's as though there should be

---

*   *"Make* every effort *to add to your faith goodness; and to goodness, knowledge; and to knowledge, self-control; and to self-control, perseverance; and to perseverance, godliness; and to godliness, brotherly kindness; and to brotherly kindness, love"* (2 Peter 1:5–7; emphasis added). Notice that the end goal is to add to our love.

no separation among us; in fact, together, we form one body, and each member belongs to all the others (Romans 12:5). Perhaps few or none of us grasp or live according to that concept to the extent God desires, but close enough to gain entrance to the place that teaches us the fullness of it, and there, we finally get it. Perhaps we *truly* treat others in heaven as we do ourselves, and we unify as one body at a level that is beyond anything done here. If that is the case (and it must be, based on Matthew 11:11 alone), how can God trust those who aren't converted to the first level of brotherhood to advance to operate by a full level of brotherhood in heaven? That further explains why only the born again—those who learn to operate by the first level—see heaven.

How to Be Born Again—Steps to Take

How do we adopt an attitude of "It's not about me, I truly care about others, and I can't outgive the Lord, anyway"? Again, we must decide to fully engage. Teetering on the edge of living a Christian life will do little or nothing to transform us to the point that our minds are renewed (Romans 12:2) to a level that we are born again. We must commit so deeply that it is akin to a marital commitment. I know, this is a scary proposition, and it was for me, but I have never seen anyone regret making that commitment. It's a good life.

Be careful not to feel like you must follow ideas of others (even some churches) for Christian living that are outside those supported by Scripture. Remember that God said not to add to His commands or take from them (Deuteronomy 4:2; see Proverbs 30:6). Focus mainly on God's two greatest commandments as declared by Jesus: *"'Love the Lord your God with all your heart and with all your soul and with all your mind.' This is the first and greatest commandment. And the second is like it: 'Love your neighbor as yourself.' All the Law and the Prophets hang on these two commandments"* (Matthew 22:37–40).

After deciding to fully engage, I recommend walking through the following five steps, all supported by Scripture, the first three regarding revamping how we think: 1) begin anew, with the openness and humility of a child; 2) quit conforming to the pattern of the world; 3) absorb the Word not as something that constrains us, but as welcomed guidance; 4) put the Word into practice; and 5) call on the assistance of the Holy Spirit. Each of these points is covered below:

1.   We Begin Anew, as Open and Humble as a Child

Jesus said in Luke 18:17, *"I tell you the truth, anyone who will not receive the kingdom of God like a little child will never enter it."* We will not overhaul how we think until we openly receive the fullness of God's message. Children don't receive a message with a critical eye—they simply receive it, and absorb it. So should we. Not only are we to receive the kingdom of God like a little child, we are to change and become like children. Jesus was clear that going to heaven depends on it: *"Unless you change and become like little children, you will never enter the kingdom of heaven"* (Matthew 18:3). (Many versions of the Bible use the words "are converted" instead of "change.") Jesus explained in the next Scripture that the greatest in heaven humbles himself like a child: *"Therefore, whoever humbles himself like this child is the greatest in the kingdom of heaven"* (Matthew 18:4). Putting these two Scriptures together, we must adopt the mindset of a child to enter heaven, and to be the greatest in heaven, we must humble ourselves like a child.

In what ways are we to change or be converted like a child? It is not explained, but we know that children, by nature and before being polluted by worldly ways, are, for the most part, dependent, trainable, trusting, not prideful, and most importantly, lowly and humble. As we "mature" in the world, we lose these innocent traits to varying degrees. Jesus provides strong warning to those of us who become confident in our own righteousness and lose our humbleness:

> To some who were confident of their own righteousness and looked down on everybody else, Jesus told this parable: "Two men went up to the temple to pray, one a Pharisee and the other a tax collector. The Pharisee stood up and prayed about himself: 'God, I thank you that I am not like other men—robbers, evildoers, adulterers—or even like this tax collector. I fast twice a week and give a tenth of all I get.' But the tax collector stood at a distance. He would not even look up to heaven, but beat his breast and said, 'God, have mercy on me, a sinner.' I tell you that this man, rather than the other, went home justified before God. For everyone who exalts himself will be humbled, and he who humbles himself will be exalted." (Luke 18:9–14)

How can God penetrate our souls if we are not humble, but are hardened with a belief that we're sufficiently righteous or that we don't need to be converted? We must put our pride aside to be converted to having a new attitude and way of thinking. Perhaps that is why pride is detestable to the Lord: *"The LORD detests all the proud of heart. Be sure of this: They will not go unpunished"* (Proverbs 16:5). Obviously, worldly pride should be avoided to the highest degree. The importance of humility was brought to light by Jesus with the following: *"Blessed are the poor in spirit, for theirs is the kingdom of heaven"* (Matthew 5:3). The "poor in spirit" are not lacking in spirit, but have the positive moral quality of humility.*

Therefore, to truly be born again as a new creation, by synthesizing these Scriptures, we begin by going back to our innocent attributes we had as a child, absorbing the Word without a critical eye, setting aside our pride, and becoming dependent (on God), trainable (by God and others), trusting (of God), and most importantly, lowly and humble. From that state of mind, the ways of God—as instructed by the Word—can reach down to the core of us. We should also crave the Word, the same as a child craves milk: *"Like newborn babies, crave spiritual milk, so that by it you may grow up in your salvation"* (1 Peter 2:2). We grow up in our salvation by becoming saturated with a new way of thinking.

2. We Quit Conforming to the Pattern of the World

After beginning anew with the openness and humility of a child, the second step in being converted is this: *"Do not conform any longer to the pattern of this world, but be transformed by the renewing of your mind"* (Romans 12:2). We don't change a little about how we think—we renew our minds. We cannot put to death our earthly nature, take off our old selves and put on the new, be born again, and become new creations with the humbleness of a child without a complete renewing of our minds to the extent that we separate ourselves from the shackles of the ways of the world. James said that one aspect of religion that God accepts as pure and faultless is to keep oneself from being polluted by the world (James 1:27).

As we soak in the Word to learn God's ways of life, we recognize how different they are from many of man's ways. Without that recognition, we will not fully know the extent of the pattern of the world with

---

*   Goodrick and Kohlenberger, *Strongest NIV Exhaustive Concordance*, s.v. "poor in spirit."

which to no longer conform, and will continue to conform to the evil desires we had when we lived in ignorance (1 Peter 1:14). And until we overcome the pattern of the world, God's commands will be burdensome (1 John 5:3–4). Our overcoming the pattern of the world is to be so complete as to be strangers here (see 1 Peter 1:17); even being friends of the world is considered hatred toward God (James 4:4).

> We cannot put to death our earthly nature, take off our old selves and put on the new, be born again, and become new creations with the humbleness of a child without a complete renewing of our minds to the extent that we separate ourselves from the shackles of the ways of the world.

We advance beyond the worldly ways of being "mere men," step by step through training, as shown by the following: *"Brothers, I could not address you as spiritual but as worldly—mere infants in Christ. I gave you milk, not solid food, for you were not yet ready for it. Indeed, you are still not ready. You are still worldly. For since there is jealousy and quarreling among you, are you not worldly? Are you not acting like mere men?"* (1 Corinthians 3:1–4). According to this Scripture, before we are ready for spiritual food, which is a more advanced level of the truth, we must quit being worldly. That is, holding on to worldly thoughts, which manifest themselves in quarreling, jealousy, and other self-absorbed ways, is an indication that we are too worldly to absorb the deeper meaning of Scripture. In fact, complaining and arguing are interferences to becoming blameless and pure: *"Do everything without complaining or arguing so that you may become blameless and pure, children of God without fault . . ."* (Philippians 2:14–15). The apostle Paul had similar instructions in 2 Timothy 2:23–24: *"Don't have anything to do with foolish and stupid arguments because you know they produce quarrels. And the Lord's servant must not quarrel."*

Reading the Word and shedding our worldly ways work together as we seek to know the full meaning of Scripture. As we remove our worldly ways, we can read a Scripture that we read before, but find a deeper understanding that we had missed. In the process, we are transformed from being mere men—being jealous, complaining, arguing, quarreling, and such—to being more godlike. Even upon advancing in spiritual maturity, we must continue to cultivate it so that it does not leave us. Paul warned us that if we think we are standing firm, we should be careful that we don't fall (1 Corinthians 10:12).

3.   We Absorb the Word as Welcomed Guidance

The third step in being converted (which is the last on the subject of changing how we think) is this: We are not to approach reading the Word simply to determine the requirements of going to heaven, but more so as a guide to know in what ways God wants us to love Him and our fellow man. In other words, seeking heaven is to be done indirectly. We seek to know how to love God and others, and heaven is the by-product of its implementation. On this subject, the apostle Paul writes,

> *So my brothers, you also died to the law through the body of Christ, that you might belong to another, to him who was raised from the dead, in order that we might bear fruit to God. For when we were controlled by the sinful nature, the sinful passions aroused by the law were at work in our bodies, so that we bore fruit for death. But now, by dying to what once bound us, we have been released from the law so that we serve in the new way of the Spirit, and not in the old way of the written code.* (Romans 7:4–6; emphasis added)

This states that we died to the law so that we might belong to Christ in order that we might bear fruit to God. That is, we are not to live for the purpose of obeying the law; we live for the purpose of belonging to Christ so that we can love and serve others, which is how we bear fruit. It also states that we are to serve in the new way of the Spirit, not in the old way of the written code.

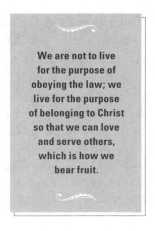

We are not to live for the purpose of obeying the law; we live for the purpose of belonging to Christ so that we can love and serve others, which is how we bear fruit.

The passage above also states that our sinful passions are actually aroused by the law. I first asked myself how that could be, but then considered our makeup as children. As many parents will attest, when we tell a child not to do something because it would be breaking a rule, the child is drawn to do that very thing. It is our makeup—for some reason, we are fascinated with the forbidden thing. The desire to do the forbidden thing is often not awakened until the child knows it is forbidden. To overcome that draw, that primitive makeup, we are to fixate our eyes on Christ and on His teaching that the foundation of the law is love. When we seek to love, and we read the Word to determine the ways in which we are to love, the Word becomes nourishment for us, as opposed to feeling bound by it.

The apostle Paul was clear that although we are not "under" law, we are to remain guided by it. The Scripture above (Romans 7:4–6) continues as follows: *"What shall we say, then? Is the law sin? Certainly not! Indeed I would not have known what sin was except through the law. For I would not have known what coveting really was if the law had not said, 'Do not covet'"* (Romans 7:7). Paul explained that no longer being under law does not open the door to allow sin: *"What then? Shall we sin because we are not under law but under grace? By no means!"* (Romans 6:15). He clarified that it is obedience that leads to righteousness (Romans 6:16), and that it is those who obey the law who will be declared righteous (Romans 2:13).

Though we are to remain guided by the law, more importantly, we look upon it differently: We are not to obey the law so that we can achieve the "score" required to go to heaven (in fact, we cannot "earn" our salvation, for we will never be good enough, and as stated before, a mind that thinks that way is of little use in heaven); instead, we lean into it because we want to know in what ways we are to love others and God, from the heart. It is *welcomed* guidance as opposed to unwelcomed confinement. We don't obey because "it's the law," we obey because we want to show our love for the Lord. We view it not as being bound by it, but led by it. We don't conquer it, we embrace it. We don't dread reading about what we are supposed to do, we lean into the words as nourishment for the soul. We don't follow God because we must, but because we are willing (see 1 Peter 5:2). In fact, we are eager to follow Him and do what is good (Titus 2:14).

This new perspective raises up a new foundation for our deeds, and they begin to flow naturally and freely from the heart, which is another means by which God's commands are not burdensome, as Jesus promised: *"For my yoke is easy and my burden is light"* (Matthew 11:30). This is our conversion, our new way of thinking that enables us to serve in the way of the Spirit, which pleases the Lord, for He weighs our hearts; our keeping the law is simply evidence of the purity of our hearts—for love. From the outflow of our deeds, our heart speaks.

This concept was missed by the Pharisees, who focused on rule-compliance without attempting to change people's inner motivations. Jesus had harsh words of rebuke for these religious leaders: *"Woe to you, teachers of the law and Pharisees, you hypocrites! You clean the outside of the* *cup and dish, but inside they are full of greed and self-indulgence. Blind Phari-see! First clean the inside of the cup and dish, and then the outside also will be clean"* (Matthew 23:25–26). The apostle Paul explained that *"circumci-sion is circumcision of the heart, by the Spirit, not by the written code"* (Romans 2:29).*

In summary, by adopting a new way of thinking, we don't just change our behavior—we become a new creation through a circumci-sion of the heart by the sanctifying work of the Holy Spirit. We have learned that *"what counts is a new creation. Peace and mercy to all who follow this rule"* (Galatians 6:15–16).

We don't just change our behavior—we become a new creation through a circumcision of the heart by the sanctifying work of the Holy Spirit.

Knowing that God asks us to convert in this way facilitates a shifting of gears within our genetic makeup, from one core part of our persona—the desire to break a rule just because it is a rule—to another core part of our persona, which we also see in every child: We are born with a desire to help. I have found that one of the most effective ways to move someone to action is to ask, "Will you help me?" Some of the sweetest words one can hear are, "You really helped me." This nourishes our spirit, for we are wired with a desire to help. Therefore, because the conversion process is simply a shift from one type of natu-ral inclination (to disobey) to another type of natural inclination (to help), it might not be as difficult as it at first seems.

If we transform our way of thinking and continue to confess our sins and re-examine whether our commitment to repent is sincere (we all continue to sin even after a conversion), we will be on the path toward godly perfection (Matthew 5:48), being transformed into His likeness (2 Corinthians 3:18). Although we will never achieve perfec-tion in this life, we will become more and more like Jesus as time goes on. As stated before, it makes sense to be in that state of advancement upon arriving in heaven, for the entrance into heaven will merely be a continuation of our path toward perfection, to be purer than we ever were on earth (Matthew 11:11; see 1 Corinthians 13:8–10).

---

* Circumcision of the heart was declared by the Lord from the beginning (See Deuteronomy 10:16 and Jeremiah 4:4), but the Pharisees did not embrace it.

4.   We Put the Word into Practice

The fourth step in being converted is to put the Word into practice. This one is easy: Simply think of ways to love others, including family, friends, co-workers, strangers, and yes, even your enemies (Luke 6:27), and ask God to bring you people who need you. He will, and you can take it from there.

5.   We Succumb to the Sanctifying Work of the Holy Spirit

The fifth and last step in being converted is to succumb to the sanctifying work of the Holy Spirit, for He helps us to be obedient (1 Peter 1:2) and to be saved (2 Thessalonians 2:13). We are born again by the assistance of the Holy Spirit: *"He saved us through the washing of rebirth and renewal by the Holy Spirit . . ."* (Titus 3:5). The Holy Spirit lives inside us and fills us up with His sanctifying work (2 Thessalonians 2:13; 1 Peter 1:2) so that He *leads us* to become sons of God. *"Those who are led by the Spirit of God are sons of God"* (Romans 8:14). How do we bring this about?

- We first decide to belong to God, and thus, we hear Him and fully understand His ways (John 8:46–47) (this was first mentioned in chapter 2 as something that cannot be overemphasized);
- We then obey God so that He will give us the Holy Spirit (Acts 5:32);
- The Holy Spirit then leads and controls us (Romans 8:6)—if we sow to please Him—to the point that we are transformed to new creations, committed to obey God.

By living according to the Holy Spirit (allowing Him to control us) and not according to our sinful nature, we meet the righteous requirements of the law (Romans 8:3–4). And because of righteousness, our spirits (not the Holy Spirit, but our own spirits) come alive: *"If Christ is in you, your body is dead because of sin, yet your spirit is alive because of righteousness"* (Romans 8:10). Putting these Scriptures together, allowing the Holy Spirit to control us causes our spirits to become alive.

Do we change ourselves, or does the Holy Spirit change us? The efforts of us and the Holy Spirit work together: *"Continue to work out your salvation with fear and trembling, for it is God who works in you to will and to act according to his good purpose"* (Philippians 2:12–13). The first part of this Scripture states that there are things for *us* to work out; the second part states that God works *in us* to bring about His purpose. Therefore, God does not do it alone, and neither do we.

I have had a few people tell me that the Holy Spirit gave them a powerful acceleration in the transformation process. One, for example, told me that he was transformed by an overwhelming feeling of oil pouring over his entire body. My minister had a similar experience: He admits to being a sinner during his young adult life (before becoming a minister), living in the flesh; but one day in church a washing came over his body that literally felt like it was raining on him. A gentleman who works for a contractor client of mine said that when he told God that he wanted to feel the Holy Spirit, he became overwhelmed with a feeling that some type of liquid was pouring through his body, which changed him. A friend of mine had an instant and overwhelming washing of peace come over him while in a fit of rage, which accelerated a change in his demeanor.

Few of us have had an accelerated experience of transformation (I haven't), but had to begin the process on our own (which is probably inspired by the Holy Spirit without our knowing it). We are to train ourselves to be godly (1 Timothy 4:7). We work in congruence with the Holy Spirit by making *every effort* to enter through the narrow door (Luke 13:24), that is, we sow to please the Spirit so that we reap eternal life. *"The one who sows to please the Spirit, from the Spirit will reap eternal life"* (Galatians 6:8). We reap eternal life *from* the Spirit, but we must sow to please the Spirit for that to occur. As we sow to please the Holy Spirit, it changes us, and at some point, it controls us (Romans 8:9–11), and we are to continue to work in congruence with the Holy Spirit until we become new creations.

As a pregnant mother should live to please the child in her, consuming good foods of high nutrition, we who are pregnant with the Holy Spirit should live to please Him in us, by consuming good foods of Christian living. The more nutrients a mother feeds to a child, the stronger he or she will be; the more nutrients we feed the Holy Spirit by sowing to please Him, the stronger He makes us spiritually, which is how *"from the Spirit, [we] will reap eternal life"* (Galatians 6:8; see John 6:63). As we sow by doing good, the Spirit makes us stronger to do good again. Operating in this way eventually leads to a complete conversion of how we think, which leads to life and peace: *"The mind of sinful man is death, but the mind controlled by the Spirit is life and peace"* (Romans 8:6).

By being converted and belonging to Jesus Christ, we crucify the sinful nature: *"Those who belong to Christ Jesus have crucified the sinful nature with its passions and desires"* (Galatians 5:24). The Holy Spirit helps us crucify or put off our sinful nature (Colossians 2:11) by permeating our being with a desire to love, from which our deeds flow in obedience to God. In other words, from the outflow of the new core of us, our obedience and deeds speak. That by-product of the fundamental change of us provides the means to hold on to the grace of salvation, and thus, the doors of heaven that were opened to us when we accepted Jesus as our Savior remain open in spite of our sins.

Even still, we are not perfect, and our sinful nature allows sin to slip through, but only occasionally, for sin is against the Spirit in us. If we fall into a pattern of deliberate sins, that is evidence that we have ignored or rejected the Holy Spirit in us and reverted to allowing the power of our sinful nature to overcome. We cannot do that. We must sow continually to please the Holy Spirit.

~10~

Are We Automatically Forgiven for Continued Sin?

People were not faithful to the old covenant, and the Lord turned away from them (Hebrews 8:9). The Lord made the new covenant with the intent that He put the laws in our minds and write them on our hearts (Hebrews 8:10) so that we can know Him, and He will remember our sins no more (Hebrews 8:12). Under the new covenant, we are justified in spite of all our sins, not like under the old covenant: *"Through him [Jesus] everyone who believes is justified from everything you could not be justified from by the law of Moses"* (Acts 13:39). Through Him, we are given a "clean slate," that is, *"everyone who believes in him receives forgiveness of sins through his name"* (Acts 10:43). We are made clean.

Remember that accepting Jesus leaves our sins committed *beforehand* unpunished (Romans 3:25). What about sins committed afterwards? Are we punished for them? Do they keep us from going to heaven? How are we forgiven for them?

Even if converted to a new person, we will continue to sin. In fact, *"if we claim to be without sin, we deceive ourselves and the truth is not in us"* (1 John 1:8). The Greek word for "sin" is *hamartia*, which means "wrongdoing, usually any act contrary to the will and law of God."* John said that *"all wrongdoing is sin"* (1 John 5:17). None of us will live completely free from deviating from the will and law of God.

---

*   Goodrick and Kohlenberger, *Strongest NIV Exhaustive Concordance*, s.v. "sin."

This chapter shows that to be forgiven for our continued sins, we are to confess them, forgive others and be merciful, not judge others, not commit the unforgivable sin, and not live according to the sinful nature. Otherwise, grace of eternal life can be taken from us. We will cover these requirements one at a time:

To Be Forgiven, We Continue to Confess Our Sins

Sins we commit after receiving knowledge of the truth are forgiven by confessing our sins: *"If we confess our sins, he is faithful and just and will forgive us our sins and purify us from all unrighteousness"* (1 John 1:9). The Greek word for "confess" is *homologeō*, which means to "confess, acknowledge, agree, admit, or declare; this can be a profession of allegiance, an admission of bad behavior, or an emphatic declaration of a truth."*

To Be Forgiven, Forgive and Be Merciful

In addition to confessing, to be forgiven also requires that we forgive others and be merciful.

One place in the New Testament instructs us to ask for forgiveness of our sins, which is in the Lord's Prayer: *"Forgive us our debts, as we*

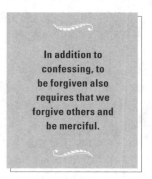

> In addition to confessing, to be forgiven also requires that we forgive others and be merciful.

also have forgiven our debtors" (Matthew 6:12). By "debts," Jesus meant "sin," as He explained in the verses immediately following the Lord's Prayer: *"For if you forgive men when they sin against you, your heavenly Father will also forgive you. But if you do not forgive men their sins, your Father will not forgive your sins"* (Matthew 6:14–15). Therefore, the Lord's forgiveness of us is limited to the extent to which we forgive others.

A similar message is conveyed in the parable of the unforgiving servant in Matthew 18:21–35. In that parable, the servant's debts (his sins) were forgiven by his master without punishment. Because the servant, however, later punished another who did

---

*   Goodrick and Kohlenberger, *Strongest NIV Exhaustive Concordance*, s.v. "confess."

not repay debts owed to him, the master revoked his forgiveness of the debts (sins) of the servant and had him punished for them.

"And when you stand praying, if you hold anything against anyone, forgive him, so that your Father in heaven may forgive you your sins" (Mark 11:25). This tells us that if we have forgiven someone, yet still hold something against that person, we haven't forgiven to the extent the Lord expects, and must forgive again. Most of us have said at some point, "I forgive him, but . . . ." We should ask ourselves if the completion of the sentence indicates that we are holding something against that person. Mercy must be complete: *"Speak and act as those who are going to be judged by the law that gives freedom, because judgment without mercy will be shown to anyone who has not been merciful. Mercy triumphs over judgment!"* (James 2:12–13). We are to be merciful, or we will receive judgment without mercy.

Forgiveness must be from the heart (Matthew 18:35), and we are to place no limit on the number of times we are to forgive: *"Then Peter came to Jesus and asked, 'Lord, how many times shall I forgive my brother when he sins against me? Up to seven times?' Jesus answered, 'I tell you, not seven times, but seventy-seven times'"* (Matthew 18:21–22; see also Luke 17:3–4).

Because we must forgive others in order to be forgiven, we should examine our hearts to see whether we are harboring *any* unforgiveness. After forgiving all whom we know we have not forgiven, I suggest taking the additional step by praying something like this:

> Lord, there is no one I can think of whom I have not forgiven, but if I haven't forgiven in the past, please forgive me for that. Lord, I declare forgiveness for anyone who has wronged me at any time, from my childhood to now. Please continue to work to soften my heart toward others.
>
> Lord, move me to love everybody, including my enemies, those who mistreat me, and those who curse me; as to all of them, replace the hardness of my heart with the softness of compassion and love, to understand that I may never understand why I am mistreated, but to pray for them. Please remind me that all of us are victims of the propensities we are born with and the experiences that we were thrust into, and that I can never judge or condemn others for their ways any more than others should judge and condemn me for my ways. Move me to purity in thought, purity in heart, and purity in actions.

We should strive to forgive with purity of heart, regardless of the level of mistreatment, the depth of injustice, or the intensity of the pain we suffer. During moments of great difficulty in forgiving, consider the level of injustice, mistreatment, and pain suffered by Jesus when He chose to forgive. He came to this earth to serve us and to save us, yet we beat Him severely and killed Him inhumanely. In the midst of that, He asked the Father to *"forgive them, for they do not know what they are doing"* (Luke 23:34). Under that perspective, is there a limit on the degree of our pain and suffering for which forgiveness of those who inflicted it should not be expected?

To Be Forgiven, Do Not Judge Others

If we pass judgment on others, we might be condemning ourselves.

- *"You, therefore, have no excuse, you who pass judgment on someone else, for at whatever point you judge the other, you are condemning yourself, because you who pass judgment do the same things"* (Romans 2:1).
- *"Do not judge, and you will not be judged. Do not condemn, and you will not be condemned. Forgive, and you will be forgiven. . . . For with the measure you use, it will be measured to you"* (Luke 6:37–38).

Luke 6:37–38 above states that the measure we use to judge others will be the Lord's measure to use when He judges us. That is, the amount of information we process about others before passing judgment on them will be the same amount of information the Lord will process about us before passing judgment on us. How many of us have been misjudged by others because they based it on too little information? Because I want God to consider all the relevant information before passing judgment on me, including the propensities I was born with and all my life experiences that molded me, I should not pass judgment on others until I have all the relevant information regarding them. Obviously, I will never have all the information, and therefore, I should never judge.

If we pass judgment on others, we might be condemning ourselves.

Another form of judging to avoid is comparing the work we do for the Lord with that done by others (Matthew 20:1–16). Also, we should not consider ourselves to be righteous, nor should we compare what we believe to be our righteousness with that of others (Luke 18:9–14). We do not know who will be first and who will be last in the kingdom of heaven: "Jesus said to them, 'I tell you the truth, the tax collectors and the prostitutes are entering the kingdom of God ahead of you. For John came to you to show you the way of righteousness, and you did not believe him, but the tax collectors and the prostitutes did'" (Matthew 21:31–32). We are not to judge a book by its cover; in fact, we are not to judge the book at all.

To Be Forgiven, Do Not Commit the Unforgivable Sin

The only single sin that is unforgivable is speaking against the Holy Spirit: *"And so I tell you, every sin and blasphemy will be forgiven men, but the blasphemy against the Spirit will not be forgiven. Anyone who speaks a word against the Son of Man will be forgiven, but anyone who speaks against the Holy Spirit will not be forgiven, either in this age or in the age to come"* (Matthew 12:31–32; see Mark 3:29; Luke 12:10). "Blasphemy" comes from the Greek word *blasph mia*, which means "slander" or "malicious talk."* "Malicious" is the adjective form of "malice." "Malice" means "a desire to harm others, or to see others suffer; ill will; spite."† "Slander" means "a false and malicious, oral statement injurious to a person's reputation."‡ Taken together, we are not to speak against the Holy Spirit with a desire to injure His name. I wish I could be more specific, but I would be guessing. I will refrain from repeating what I have read as to what others concluded regarding this question because they were guessing.

To Be Forgiven, Do Not Sow to Please the Sinful Nature

If we sow to please our sinful nature, we lose grace of eternal life: *"The one who sows to please his sinful nature, from that nature will reap destruction; the one who sows to please the Spirit, from the Spirit will reap eternal life"* (Galatians 6:8). Inside of us is a sinful nature. Also inside us is

---

* Goodrick and Kohlenberger, *Strongest NIV Exhaustive Concordance*, s.v. "blasphemy."
† *The American Heritage Dictionary*, 2007.
‡ Ibid.

the Holy Spirit if we love God and obey His teaching (John 14:23–24; Acts 5:32; 1 John 3:24), if we acknowledge that Jesus is the Son of God (1 John 4:15), and if we love others (1 John 4:12). Galatians 6:8 tells us that it is not the sinful nature in us, by itself, that will lead us to destruction, but the sowing to please it, and conversely, it is not the Spirit inside us, by Himself, that will reap eternal life, but the sowing to please Him. We nourish one or the other, which is our choice.

Sowing to please the sinful nature insults God's love for us so much that it is like trampling on His Son:

> If we deliberately keep on sinning after we have received the knowledge of the truth, no sacrifice for sins is left, but only a fearful expectation of judgment and of raging fire that will consume the enemies of God. Anyone who rejected the law of Moses died without mercy on the testimony of two or three witnesses. How much more severely do you think a man deserves to be punished who has trampled the Son of God underfoot, who has treated as an unholy thing the blood of the covenant that sanctified him, and who has insulted the Spirit of grace? For we know him who said, "It is mine to avenge; I will repay," and again, "The Lord will judge his people." It is a dreadful thing to fall into the hands of the living God. (Hebrews 10:26–31)

The message here is that those who rejected the law under the old covenant died without mercy, and under the new covenant, it is even more of a rejection to deliberately keep on sinning: We are considered enemies of God, and therefore, dying without mercy is not enough—God will repay. When we deliberately keep on sinning, we reject the sacrifice Jesus made for sins, and thus, reject the grace of eternal life. Hebrews 6:4–6 tells us that if we fall away, it is impossible to be brought back into repentance because we are crucifying the Son of God all over again and subjecting Him to public disgrace. Peter warned that by turning our backs on the sacred command, we are worse off at the end than we were at the beginning (2 Peter 2:20–22).

If we claim to truly believe in Jesus, we will not go on sinning anyway. That is surmised by combining the next two Scriptures: *"Everyone who believes that Jesus is the Christ is born of God"* (1 John 5:1). *"No one who is born of God will continue to sin, because God's seed remains in him; he cannot go on sinning, because he has been born of God"* (1 John 3:9; emphasis added). Also, if we claim to know Jesus or live in Him, we cannot keep on sinning: *"No one who lives in him [Jesus] keeps on sinning. No one*

who continues to sin has either seen him or known him" (1 John 3:6). Therefore, if we go on sinning, we do not believe that Jesus is the Christ.
These Scriptures and Hebrews 10:26–31 are
also consistent with Scripture that states that
we must obey in order to go to heaven (Matthew 7:21; 19:17; Luke 10:25–28, in combi-
nation with John 8:31–32; 12:50; Hebrews
5:8–10; 1 John 2:17; 5:2).

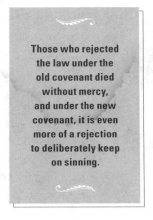

Those who rejected
the law under the
old covenant died
without mercy,
and under the new
covenant, it is even
more of a rejection
to deliberately keep
on sinning.

But does this mean that if we sin, even one
time, we will lose grace of eternal life? That is
hard to believe, considering that we all sin. In
fact, the apostle John stated in 1 John 1:8 that
if we claim to be without sin, we deceive ourselves and the truth is not in us. Therefore,
the answer has to be "no," which is confirmed
by the apostle John: *"I write this to you so that you will not sin. But if anybody
does sin, we have one who speaks to the Father in our defense—Jesus Christ, the
Righteous One. He is the atoning sacrifice for our sins"* (1 John 2:1–2). John
also said the following: *"If we confess our sins, he is faithful and just and will
forgive us our sins and purify us from all unrighteousness"* (1 John 1:9). But
how do we reconcile that with the statement in Hebrews 10:26 that if
we deliberately keep on sinning, we are enemies of God who can expect
judgment and raging fire, and with 1 John 3:9, which states that if we
are born of God, we cannot go on sinning?

A closer look reveals that the words used are not as to one sin, but
a number of them: *"go on sinning"* is in 1 John 3:9, and *"deliberately keep
on sinning"* is in Hebrews 10:26–31. The question then becomes: How
many deliberate sins are will cause us to lose grace of eternal life? The
Bible does not indicate anything specifically by number or magnitude,
but it does provide guideposts:

- Is my heart always going astray? (Hebrews 3:7–11)
- According to what pattern am I living? (Philippians 3:17)
- Am I self-seeking and following evil? (Romans 2:8)
- Is my sin "full-grown"? (James 1:15)
- Do I "indulge the sinful nature"? (Galatians 5:13)
- Do I "live according to the sinful nature"? (Romans 8:13)
- Do I conform to the evil desires I had when I lived in ignorance?
  (1 Peter 1:14)

- Do I "follow the corrupt desire of the sinful nature"? (2 Peter 2:4–10)
- Do I sow to please my sinful nature? (Galatians 6:8)
- Am I "controlled by the sinful nature"? (Romans 8:8)

Or . . .

- Do I persist in doing good? (Romans 2:7)
- Am I "led by the Spirit of God"? (Romans 8:14; Galatians 5:18)
- Do I live "according to the Spirit"? (Romans 8:4)
- Have I put off the sinful nature? (Colossians 2:11)
- Do I restrain sensual indulgence? (Colossians 2:23)
- Am I "eager to do what is good"? (Titus 2:14)
- Do I have a "pledge of a good conscience toward God"? (1 Peter 3:21)
- Do I sow to please the Spirit? (Galatians 6:8)
- Is my "mind controlled by the Spirit"? (Romans 8:6)

Based on the above, the broadest question in determining if our continued deliberate sinning is of the degree that we lose grace of eternal life is this: Are we living according to our sinful nature? Those who are will not go to heaven. This is not to say, however, that deliberate sins here and there are our destruction, because there is a difference between sowing to please the sinful nature and the occasional lapse of allowing the sinful nature within us to have its way. As stated before, all of us sin, and we never quit sinning (1 John 1:10), and if we confess our sins, they will be forgiven as promised in 1 John 1:9.

This probably comes as a surprise to those who follow a watered-down teaching of the Bible, but it should not be a surprise to those who know the Bible well. In fact, sinning defiantly had the same consequence in the old covenant. One who sinned unintentionally was required to bring an animal for a sin offering, and when atonement was made, he was forgiven (Numbers 15:27). Defiant sinning, however, was not forgiven: *"But anyone who sins defiantly, whether native-born or alien, blasphemes the LORD, and that person must be cut off from his people. Because he has despised the LORD's word and broken his commands, that person must surely be cut off; his guilt remains on him"* (Numbers 15:30–31).

Based on Hebrews 10:26–31, the Lord takes even greater offense to deliberate sins committed under the new covenant. It states that anyone who rejected the law of Moses died without mercy, but *"how much more severely do you think a man deserves to be punished who has trampled the Son of God under foot, who has treated as an unholy thing the blood of the covenant that sanctified him, and who has insulted the Spirit of grace?"* Jesus did not die for anyone under the old covenant, and He did under the new, and therefore sin under the new covenant—a rejection of that sacrifice—is more offensive to the Lord than blaspheming His name as stated in Numbers 15:30–31. By the blood of Jesus, we were "bought at a price" (1 Corinthians 6:20), and we are expected to act accordingly.

In my study and research in writing this book, perhaps the most alarming part was learning the depth to which the Lord takes offense to a pattern of deliberate sin after Christ died for the forgiveness of sin. Even before we were bought at a price, repeated backsliding was subject to serious repercussions: *"'You have rejected me,' declares the LORD. 'You keep on backsliding. So I will lay hands on you and destroy you; I can no longer show compassion'"* (Jeremiah 15:6). How much more serious is continued backsliding after Christ died for us? Why do we act as though those Scriptures are not in the Bible? In a society where fear of the Lord has virtually become a forgotten attribute, have we also forgotten that the Lord punishes sin? If our friends are living the same sinful ways as we are, and no one is admonishing anyone, does that mean the Lord thinks it is not so bad?

It is utterly foolish to ignore Scripture on how God views sin: Sin is hostile to God (Romans 8:7); it alienates us from Him (Colossians 1:21); God grieves when we rebel (Isaiah 63:10); our sins and offenses burden and weary Him (Isaiah 43:24) and cause Him to hide His face from us (Isaiah 59:2); our iniquities separate us from Him (Isaiah 59:2), and our sins make us waste away (Isaiah 64:7; Jeremiah 33:5). Sin can bring God's wrath on us (Romans 1:18; 2:8; 13:4; Colossians 3:6; Ephesians 5:6; Hebrews 10:26–31). In fact, every disobedience will receive its just punishment (Hebrews 2:2). On Judgment Day, we will receive what is due us for the things we did, whether good or bad (2 Corinthians 5:10).

> In a society where fear of the Lord has virtually become a forgotten attribute, have we also forgotten that the Lord punishes sin?

The Lord punishes us individually for sin (Matthew 18:35; 25:46; Luke 12:47; Romans 1:27, 13:4; 1 Thessalonians 4:6; 2 Peter 2:9), and for certain sins, we will be punished most severely (Mark 12:40).

Also, severe punishment awaits those who deliberately keep on sinning after receiving the knowledge of the truth (Hebrews 10:26–31). (Examples in the Old Testament of the Lord's punishment of individuals for sin are so many that they are not listed here.)

The Lord also punishes a nation for sin: *"'But if any nation does not listen, I will completely uproot and destroy it,' declares the LORD"* (Jeremiah 12:17). *"In a similar way, Sodom and Gomorrah and the surrounding towns gave themselves up to sexual immorality and perversion. They serve as an example of those who suffer the punishment of eternal fire"* (Jude 1:7). *"Cut down the trees and build siege ramps against Jerusalem. This city must be punished; it is filled with oppression"* (Jeremiah 6:6). In response to sin, the Lord might simply choose to hide His face: *"I will hide my face from this city because of all its wickedness"* (Jeremiah 33:5).

We have learned that receiving grace of eternal life is easy, which was not the case under the old covenant. We also learned that we are to focus on love, with the law to guide us on how to love, and that we are to love at a high level: We are to love our neighbor as much as we love ourselves. That also is required in the old covenant (Leviticus 19:18). Yet Hebrews 10:26–31 makes it clear that deliberate sin is considered worse by the Lord under the new covenant than under the old. Because of the emphasis churches place on grace, I used to think that all aspects of the new covenant were relaxed; this is not so regarding the laws of love— under those laws, we are now held to a higher standard of obedience.

Ways to Cover Over Sins

Because we all sin, we should seek to do the following, which can cover over a multitude of sins:

- *"Above all, love each other deeply, because love covers over a multitude of sins"* (1 Peter 4:8).
- *"My brothers, if one of you should wander from the truth and someone should bring him back, remember this: Whoever turns a sinner from the error of his way will save him from death and cover over a multitude of sins"* (James 5:19–20).

When I feel bad about disappointing God in some way, I have the comfort of knowing that I can make up for it by loving others and turning a sinner from the error of his way. The importance of these two Scriptures, being the only ones that tell us how to cover over a multitude of sins, should not be forgotten.

In summary of this chapter, if we blaspheme the Holy Spirit, we will not be forgiven (Matthew 12:31–32; Mark 3:29; Luke 12:10). Also, if we deliberately continue to sin after receiving knowledge of the truth, that is evidence of whose power we've chosen to be under, that we're being "controlled by the sinful nature," which will put us in the throes of a fearful expectation of judgment and of raging fire that will consume the enemies of God (Hebrews 10:26–31). By turning our backs on the sacred command, we are worse off at the end than we were at the beginning (2 Peter 2:20–22). If, however, we sow to please the Spirit, from the Spirit we will reap eternal life (Galatians 6:8). We have our mind

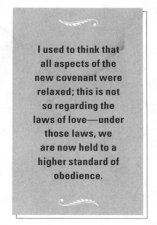

I used to think that all aspects of the new covenant were relaxed; this is not so regarding the laws of love—under those laws, we are now held to a higher standard of obedience.

set on what the Spirit desires (Romans 8:3–4) and will not fall from grace of eternal life. We will continue to sin, for all of us sin (1 John 1:10), but we will not live in a pattern of sin (Philippians 3:17). For those sins we commit, if we confess, He will forgive us and purify us from all unrighteousness (1 John 1:9), provided that we also forgive others (Matthew 6:14–15; 18:35; Mark 11:25), are merciful (James 2:12–13), and do not judge others (Luke 6:37–38; Romans 2:1), for the measure we use when judging others will be the measure God will use when He judges us (Luke 6:37–38). We should also seek to cover over sins by loving each other deeply (1 Peter 4:8) and by turning sinners from the errors of their ways (James 5:19–20).

God loves us as much as He loves His own Son (John 17:23), and His love for us endures forever (Psalm 136:1–26). I can think of a love no greater than that of God when He sent His only Son to be tortured and to die so that all of us could be reconciled to Him. To what depth would I have to love another to bring me to a willingness to sacrifice my son in that way? To what depth am I willing to demonstrate my love to God by obeying Him?

When my wife, Tamara, passed away, I was assaulted with the reality that in an instant, a person's worldly possessions turn to nothing. Tamara's beautiful clothes were worthless. Our lovely home she would never see again. That shock was the beginning of a richer focus—my thoughts turned toward heaven. Immersing myself in Scripture enlightened me to the essence of what Jesus is telling us: This earth is only a training ground to convert us from selfishness to selflessness so that we do not fall away from God's grace of eternal life. This life is joyful to me, but in comparison to heaven, it's nothing. This life is not the "meat and potatoes." It's not even the appetizer. It's merely a testing ground to see if I love God and others enough to be transformed from my natural inclination to gather and guard my crumbs to share my crumbs (all my luxuries are crumbs when compared to heaven); if I pass the test, I will wake up one day and be ushered into a feast. That is the true life which I should "in my joy" give up my crumbs to attain (Matthew 13:44–46).

> I can think of a love no greater than that of God when He sent His only Son to be tortured and to die so that all of us could be reconciled to Him.

~ 11 ~

It Is Never Too Late to Be Saved

Grace is granted freely and easily—that is, nothing is required of us other than believing in Jesus. Through the Lord Jesus Christ, we are washed, sanctified, and justified (1 Corinthians 6:9–11).

A beautiful aspect of grace is that it's never too late to be saved, and it is no less available to the worst sinner than to those who devoted their entire lives to obeying God.

We Can Be Saved Just Before Death

The following Scripture passage shows how freely grace is given. It occurs while Jesus is hanging on the cross between two criminals on their respective crosses:

> One of the criminals who hung there hurled insults at him: "Aren't you the Christ? Save yourself and us!"
>
> But the other criminal rebuked him. "Don't you fear God," he said, "since you are under the same sentence? We are punished justly, for we are getting what our deeds deserve. But this man has done nothing wrong."
>
> Then he said, "Jesus, remember me when you come into your kingdom."
>
> Jesus answered him, "I tell you the truth, today you will be with me in paradise." (Luke 23:39–43)

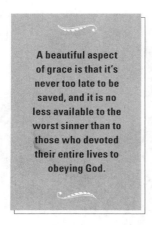

A beautiful aspect of grace is that it's never too late to be saved, and it is no less available to the worst sinner than to those who devoted their entire lives to obeying God.

The thief on the cross merely made a statement that showed that he believed Jesus Christ was the Son of God. Even for a convicted and admitted criminal, nothing more was required. Through Jesus, we are justified freely by grace (Romans 3:23–24). After grace is given, however, nothing in the Bible states that we are free to sin afterwards. Had the criminal lived longer, as explained earlier in this book, he would have lost that justification had he not lived as a committed believer.

The next parable, declared by Jesus as an example of what the kingdom of heaven is like, shows that the same heavenly blessings await us whether we come to the Lord late in life or early.

"For the kingdom of heaven is like a landowner who went out early in the morning to hire men to work in his vineyard. He agreed to pay them a denarius for the day and sent them into his vineyard.

"About the third hour he went out and saw others standing in the marketplace doing nothing. He told them, 'You also go and work in my vineyard, and I will pay you whatever is right.' So they went.

"He went out again about the sixth hour and the ninth hour and did the same thing. About the eleventh hour he went out and found still others standing around. He asked them. 'Why have you been standing here all day long doing nothing?'

"'Because no one has hired us,' they answered.

"He said to them, 'You also go and work in my vineyard.'

"When evening came, the owner of the vineyard said to his foreman, 'Call the workers and pay them their wages, beginning with the last ones hired and going on to the first.'

"The workers who were hired about the eleventh hour came and each received a denarius. So when those came who were hired first, they expected to receive more. But each one of them also received a denarius. When they received it, they began to grumble against the landowner. 'These men who were hired last worked only one hour,' they said, 'and you have made them equal to us who have borne the burden of the work and the heat of the day.'

"But he answered one of them, 'Friend, I am not being unfair to you. Didn't you agree to work for a denarius? Take your pay and go. I want to give the man who was hired last the same as I gave you. Don't I have the

right to do what I want with my own money? Or are you envious because I am generous?'

"So the last will be first, and the first will be last" (Matthew 20:1–16).

The criminal who was granted eternal life while hanging on the cross showed his belief in Jesus at the last hour, and he received the same reward as those who follow Christ all their lives. The parable above confirms that the reward of heaven is the same for all, and it teaches us to not compare our time of serving Jesus to that of others. After all, none of us are good enough to go; it is by God's grace that we go, and we should not envy others who received grace at the last hour.

The Lord is thrilled when anyone is saved, and so should we be. In fact, the Lord might be even more thrilled over a person coming to Him who had lived a wayward life over one who was always with Him. That is illustrated in the parable of the lost son, whose father celebrated more over the return of his son who lived a life of sin than the son whose life was committed to him always (Luke 15:11–31).

There is a warning from Jesus, however, for those who choose to wait to the last hour to prepare for heaven, for no one knows when he or she will pass away:

> *"[T]he kingdom of heaven will be like ten virgins who took their lamps and went out to meet the bridegroom. Five of them were foolish and five were wise. The foolish ones took their lamps but did not take any oil with them. The wise, however, took oil in jars along with their lamps. The bridegroom was a long time in coming, and they all became drowsy and fell asleep.*
>
> *"At midnight the cry rang out: 'Here's the bridegroom! Come out to meet him!'*
>
> *"Then all the virgins woke up and trimmed their lamps. The foolish ones said to the wise, 'Give us some of your oil; our lamps are going out.'*
>
> *"'No,' they replied, 'there may not be enough for both us and you. Instead, go to those who sell oil and buy some for yourselves.'*
>
> *"But while they were on their way to buy the oil, the bridegroom arrived. The virgins who were ready went in with him to the wedding banquet. And the door was shut.*
>
> *"Later the others also came. 'Sir! Sir!' they said. 'Open the door for us!'*
>
> *"But he replied, 'I tell you the truth, I don't know you.'*
>
> *"Therefore keep watch because you do not know the day or the hour"*

(Matthew 25:1–13).

No Prequalification to Receive God's Grace

There is no prequalification to receiving God's grace. *"For God so loved the world that he gave his one and only Son, that whoever believes in him shall not perish but have eternal life"* (John 3:16). Notice that Jesus does not say "for God so loved the righteous" or "for God so loved the elect" or "for God so loved all but the worst sinners." Nothing indicates that the "world" includes less than all of us. (For more on this topic, see the section titled "God Wants All to Be Saved" in chapter 2.)

There is no prequalification to receiving God's grace.

I once heard of a lady who said she could not ask to be saved because she had lived a life that was entirely too undeserving. Oh, how wrong she was. The degree of our sins before receiving God's grace is irrelevant. Jesus' parable in Matthew 18:21–35 shows that even an enormous amount of sins will be forgiven. In fact, *"where sin increased, grace increased all the more"* (Romans 5:20). Also, the greater our sins have been, the greater will be our love to God after we are forgiven (Luke 7:36–50), and we have learned that we must love the Lord our God to go to heaven.

~12~

Final Thoughts

After losing Tamara and seeking to become closer to the Lord, I picked a day in the future on which I would make a promise to God to do my best to live in full accordance with Scripture. It was a day of a special church service, and there, I met one of the leaders who was told about my commitment. He looked at me and said, calmly and confidently, "It's a good life." Those were soothing words, because I was apprehensive and concerned that if I enjoyed my life less as a result, I might regret my decision. As I write this, I have been living this new life for seven years, and I endorse that gentleman's words, "It's a good life."

What's good about it? First, living in wonder as to whether I'm going to heaven has been removed, which is very comforting. Second, I know that God can fix anything and that He works for my good: *"God works for the good of those who love him, who have been called according to his purpose"* (Romans 8:28), and if we *"commit to the LORD whatever [we] do, [our] plans will succeed"* (Proverbs 16:3). Frankly, I would be scared to death at times if I thought I did not have the Lord's protection, and I sometimes wonder how others can cope under the belief that they don't have it. Third, getting out of the "it's about me" way of thinking is liberating. Walking through life believing that "it's about me" can fuel some of the attributes of my sin nature as described in Galatians 5:19–21 (*"sexual immorality, impurity and debauchery; idolatry and witchcraft; hatred, discord, jealousy, fits of rage, selfish ambition, dissensions, factions, and envy;*

drunkenness, orgies, and the like"). For example, hatred comes from feeling that someone mistreated me. Envy comes from thinking someone else has more than I do, and jealously comes from believing that my having less is unjust. Fits of rage come from feeling that someone mistreated me. Selfish ambition comes from desiring more material things to hoard for myself. Discord is fueled by seeking my own needs. Impurity comes from seeking unclean pleasures and passions.

This heavy sludge is removed when I make myself last (in addition to the fact that these self-centered attributes remove the kingdom of God from me [Galatians 5:21]). When living as though life is not about me, it is easier to turn the other cheek, pray for my enemies, walk in forgiveness, be content with what I have, give generously, and walk in love. Indeed, the Christian life is more joyful.

Do Not Fall Away

Once we align ourselves with Jesus, we must try to be, as C.S. Lewis describes it, "a little Jesus." We carry the badge of Christianity, and we cannot give it a bad name. Temptations can dangerously draw us to fall away from the Lord. One of the greatest temptations that can move us away from Christian principles is when upholding them threatens the perceived security that money offers. I have often told my son that one of the greatest tests of a man's character is when upholding it costs a good bit of money. For example, if I hit another car in a parking lot, do I leave a note with my name and phone number even though I know that I won't get caught if I drive away? If I fail that test, how is that different from stealing, for I have imposed upon an innocent person an expense that I should have borne? Though indirectly, I took from him or her, which is as bad as stealing a person's wallet from the seat of an unlocked car.

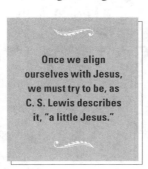

Once we align ourselves with Jesus, we must try to be, as C. S. Lewis describes it, "a little Jesus."

As another example, as a professional, if I make an error that clearly costs my client a good bit of money, but he does not know it unless I tell him, have I stolen from him by not confessing and paying for the loss myself? I believe that, for almost all of us, the extent to which we pass this test is in direct proportion to the amount of money involved.

How much is our character worth? For how much are we willing to sell our soul? Our soul and character are priceless, and we should never fail the test of weighing their value against the cost of maintaining it. When we are tempted in these situations, God will provide a way out so that we can stand up under it. *"No temptation has seized you except what is common to man. And God is faithful; he will not let you be tempted beyond what you can bear. But when you are tempted, he will also provide a way out so that you can stand up under it"* (1 Corinthians 10:13). Even without this Scripture to lean on, why in the world would we believe that our lives would be worse off by passing these types of tests, and how in the world can we be better off if we fail those tests and, in essence, steal from others? God is watching. We must know that God's wrath will come on us when we harm others, and trust that His protection will come on us when we help others.

"So do not throw away your confidence; it will be richly rewarded. You need to persevere so that when you have done the will of God, you will receive what he has promised. For in just a very little while, 'He who is coming will come and will not delay. But my righteous one will live by faith. And if he shrinks back, I will not be pleased with him.' But we are not of those who shrink back and are destroyed, but of those who believe and are saved" (Hebrews 10:35–39). I will say it again: God is watching. All that we do should be done with that in mind.

Help Others Not to Fall Away

In addition to guarding ourselves from turning our backs on Christianity, we are to help others in that regard. Correcting someone is even better than flattery: *"He who rebukes a man will in the end gain more favor than he who has a flattering tongue"* (Proverbs 29:23). We need to be careful, however, not to judge or condemn. But if another is clearly sinning, we should strongly consider exposing the light of God's ways to that person, for *"whoever turns a sinner from the error of his way will save him from death and cover over a multitude of sins"* (James 5:20). Also, *"if someone is caught in a sin, you who are spiritual should* restore *him gently. But watch yourself, or you also may be tempted. Carry each other's burdens, and in this way you will fulfill the law of Christ"* (Galatians 6:1–2; emphasis added).

This is easier said than done. Our manner of approach is very important. I like the word "restore" in this verse. It's interesting that it includes a command to carry each other's burdens. Perhaps someone who is "caught in a sin" has been tempted because upon his or her shoulders many burdens have been placed. To assist that person by restoring him or her gently, an option might be to help carry that person's burdens. What an example that would be in our efforts to restore that person to align himself or herself with Christian principles. Overall, though, turning a sinner from the error of his way should be done with love, and not with a condemning attitude.

> **Turning a sinner from the error of his way should be done with love, and not with a condemning attitude.**

Remember that the Scripture above says to restore him *gently*.

We should also be careful not to convey to others an interpretation of Scripture that forbids an act that is not clearly forbidden, or that requires an act that is not required, but is a man-made rule (Deuteronomy 4:2; see Proverbs 30:6). For example, some denominations believe we are not to drink alcohol. Scripture says we are not to get drunk on wine, which leads to debauchery (Ephesians 5:18), and acts of a sinful nature include drunkenness (Galatians 5:21), but drinking wine or other alcohol is not forbidden; we simply are not to drink to excess.

We should be prepared to receive correction when we fall away in some areas. In fact, we should *hope* that someone would love us enough to restore us gently and turn us from the error of our way. When it happens, know that a person who does that is putting his or her relationship at risk in an attempt to help. It is easier for the person to simply turn his or her head—out of laziness, not caring, or fear of rejection—and choose not to help. Therefore, it is immature and unwise to be offended by someone's attempt to help us through correction. *"Do not rebuke a mocker or he will hate you; rebuke a wise man and he will love you"* (Proverbs 9:8). Be wise—love those who rebuke you.

Do Not Be Discouraged

"Let us not become weary in doing good, for at the proper time we will reap a harvest if we do not give up. Therefore, as we have opportunity, let us do good to all people, especially to those who belong to the family of believers" (Galatians 6:9–10).

Try not to be discouraged if you see other Christians falter, but stay the course of good living yourself. All of us have failures, in part because Satan pushes Christians to fail. We cannot allow Satan a second victory by allowing us to get down on Christianity as a result of his victories over Christians.

Trust the Lord

The pinnacle of freedom is in reaching a level of maturity in our faith that we rejoice in everything, for that is faith unadulterated; it is a state of little or no anxiety, which is achieved under the comfort of knowing that God is in control, that we are under His protection. Then the challenges of following His will are not so challenging; the trials and tribulations of life are viewed no longer as frustrating interferences, but as part of the plan, the development into Christian maturity.

This level of maturity is very difficult to reach and more difficult to maintain. I have been protected by the Lord so often and in so many ways, yet I still find myself in a state of worry at times, though much less frequently and to a lesser degree because of where I have advanced in the Lord in recent years. A state of concern is good, for it motivates me to take action; a state of worry beyond a minimal level, however, shows a lack of faith (expecting a complete lack of worry is not realistic).

We should remind ourselves that grace is sometimes revealed through hardships (2 Corinthians 12:7–10), which, by us enduring them and being trained by them (Hebrews 12:10–11), bring us to a deeper level of maturity and character (Romans 5:3–4). We should never forget that there is a time for everything—a time for correction through hardships, a time for financial blessings, and a time for other forms of God's grace, all being doled out in accordance with His will, under His infinite wisdom. We should live under the knowing of God's protection. *"God has said, 'Never will I leave you; never will I forsake you'"*(Hebrews 13:5). *"Therefore, my dear brothers, stand firm. Let nothing move you. Always give yourselves fully to the work of the Lord, because you know that your labor in the Lord is not in vain"* (1 Corinthians 15:58).

Do Not Hide Jesus

"Whoever acknowledges me before men, I will also acknowledge him before my Father in heaven. But whoever disowns me before men, I will disown him before

my Father in heaven" (Matthew 10:32–33). *"If anyone is ashamed of me and my words in this adulterous and sinful generation, the Son of Man will be ashamed of him when he comes in his Father's glory with the holy angels"* (Mark 8:38). This is a warning to those who succumb to pressure to not offend those of non-Christian religions by hiding their allegiance to Jesus.

To sell my house, I hired a staging consultant to recommend ways to dress it up by rearranging furniture and accessories in order to appeal to potential buyers. She recommended that I put away displays of the cross, believing that it might make a potential buyer uncomfortable. I will never hurt Jesus that way! He died for me. Am I really going to hide the symbol of His sacrifice in order to not offend someone who rejected that sacrifice for himself or herself?

Enjoy the Journey

We are not here to be martyrs. To the contrary, I have found that doing our best to live in full accordance with Scripture brings fresh air and enrichment to our lives here, which should carry on to the next life in heaven.

In our quest to do what it takes to go to heaven, may our journey never end. When seeking to be transformed into the likeness of the Lord with ever-increasing glory, may our journey never end. The beauty is in the journey itself. On that journey, ask for the Lord's assistance, and learn to rely on Him only. Whether Christians or not, people will frequently let us down, but we should try hard to never grow weary. Always live in love no matter the circumstances, for love never fails. Cast away bitterness and unforgiveness, which is a cancer to the soul. Embrace trials and tribulations as opportunities for growth, for pruning and shedding, and for fine-tuning your heart for deeper levels of love. Remember that on God, you can always depend.

All we do should be in the context of what it takes to go to heaven, for not much matters on earth anyway.

All we do should be in the context of what it takes to go to heaven, for not much matters on earth anyway. At all times, look up, for our citizenship is somewhere up there in the big sky, in the place of paradise that God's grace has bestowed upon us.

Stay the course and hold fast to the thought that your mind and spirit will never die, that you will simply awake one day to find that both are housed in a different body, which will never die. The only thing we take with us is that which we give away, and the most blessed gift we can leave here is the assurance with our loved ones that we are entering the precious everlasting life, enlightened with the anticipation of reuniting someday with all of them to grow in deeper levels of love. Yes, the beauty is in the journey and in knowing that each new day brings continued growth, not just in this life, but in the afterlife. May your journey to heaven begin now, and may a sprinkling of it come to you while here, and continue in greater doses as the journey continues.

When you arrive, look me up. We'll celebrate your arrival over a cup of coffee and do a high five over discovering the greater mysteries of Christianity and the multiple layers of beauty that God will be revealing to us.

Many blessings to you all!

~ Epilogue ~

A Letter from Heaven

If my late wife could write a letter to me, this is what I think she would say:

My darling Tim,

I love you from the deepest part of my heart. You were the darling of my life. Although it broke my heart when we separated in the flesh, it was so precious to arrive here. *"Precious in the sight of the LORD is the death of his saints"* (Psalm 116:15). My passing away from the earth is precious to the Lord because it's precious to me. In heaven, there is no longing, no pain, no sorrow, no disappointment, and no wishing for anything. There is such love, a love that is so pure and permeating that it fills the air with its sweet aroma. There is such joy, a joy that is so deep that it fills every portal to my soul, leaving room for nothing else. It is impossible to adequately convey to you the level of ecstasy and exceeding wonder that I and all others here experience each moment. It is a new dimension of existence that no earthly words can explain, but I will attempt to do so.

Love abounds and penetrates through and among all of us, and there is no separation between us, nor with God and our Lord Jesus Christ. My immeasurable level of joy and peace flows and spreads so freely—it cannot be contained within my heavenly body, which is a resemblance of my earthly body, only better, but without earthly flesh. All of us together form the body of Christ, without boundaries between us, for the Spirit flows among and through us. All of us, together, comprise but one spirit, and therefore, as we do for others, we do for ourselves.

Consequently, the level of love, intimacy, and joy penetrates my soul in a way that is deeper than anything I experienced on earth.

On Judgment Day, our Lord Jesus Christ explained all Scripture to me, and for the first time, the whole truth of the fullness of God's love became clear and transparent. On earth, I understood it only within the limited earthly bounds of my mind, through the filter of the deceptiveness of worldly ways. I am so grateful that, while there, I chose to simply rely on faith, on the unseen, living in love as best I knew how.

God told me that He was so pleased, as obviously was I, that I always had your dedication, your commitment, and your love. I had your entire heart. He told me that He longed to receive those same depths of your heart in your relationship with Him. He said that when I passed, you were more open to receive the fullness of Him than at any time before, and He was going to send people to assist you in going deeper with Him. I am so grateful that He was so patient with you.

Recently, God expressed to me His joy that you allowed Him to capture and consume your entire heart, which brings me such joy, because nothing there matters; all that matters is what's up here, and it lasts for an eternity. *"So we fix our eyes not on what is seen, but on what is unseen. For what is seen is temporary, but what is unseen is eternal"* (2 Corinthians 4:18). You, Tim, have fixed your eyes on what is unseen, and I can't wait for you to see it!

I fully understand now that Scripture is written beautifully, completely, and perfectly. Please continue to immerse yourself in the Word, believing everything and absorbing the greater depth of the truth. I am precluded from conveying to you the complete truth, for God yearns for all to learn that on their own through studying, meditating on, and living the Word.

My precious Tim, I pray for you to be obedient so that God's good, pleasing, and perfect will can be done. I pray for you to be cheerful and joyful so that you will want for nothing, to share so that it will be given to you, to be compassionate so that compassion will abound to you, to show mercy so that mercy follows you, to forgive so that you will be forgiven, to love so that you will receive eternal love, to throw away self so that you can have, and to throw down your life so that you can truly live. The yoke is indeed light for those who live by these principles.

Please convey my deepest love to my girls, John-Michael, my mother, my brother, my remaining family, and my friends. Please spread the Word of truth to them and to all those you encounter. Believe everything in Scripture—everything.

Until we reunite in this full presence of paradise, I will be with you always in spirit. My love for you transcends all understanding. It will be so very beautiful when you arrive, my darling Tim, when my hands join yours, together with the hands of Jesus, when your name is called to receive what awaits you for the way you lived out your faith—in love. You and I will be united again in Christ, but this time for eternity, in our home of paradise! I can't wait to see you, my sweet darling!

Forever,
Tamara

Bibliography

Aldridge, Faye. *Real Messages from Heaven*. Lebanon, TN: Davis Jackson Publishers, 2012.

Barclay, William. *The Gospel of Matthew*, Part 2. Rev. ed. Philadelphia: Westminster, 1975.

Bruner, Frederick Dale. *Matthew: A Commentary*, vol. 2. Grand Rapids: Eerdmans, 1990.

Piper, Don, with Cecil Murphey. *90 Minutes in Heaven*. Grand Rapids: Fleming H. Revell, 2004.

Prince, Dennis and Nolene. *Nine Days in Heaven*. Lake Mary, FL: Creation House, 2006.

Springer, Rebecca. *Within Heaven's Gates*. New Kensington, PA: Whitaker House, 1984.

Wiese, Bill. *23 Minutes in Hell*. Lake Mary, FL: Charisma House, 2006.

Scripture Index

Page numbers with "n" means Scripture is found in the footnote of the designated page.

Genesis 1:26   *7n, 68*
Genesis 6:6   *68*

Exodus 9:12   *8n*
Exodus 20:5   *68*
Exodus 32:12   *60n*
Exodus 34:14   *68*

Leviticus 19:18   *94, 148*
Leviticus 27:30–32   *108*

Numbers 15:27   *146*
Numbers 15:30–31   *146, 147*
Numbers 21:16   *8n*

Deuteronomy 4:2   *11, 118, 129, 158*
Deuteronomy 10:16   *135n*
Deuteronomy 14:22   *107*
Deuteronomy 15:10   *124*
Deuteronomy 28:45   *60n*
Deuteronomy 28:62–63   *60n*
Deuteronomy 32:4   *12*
Deuteronomy 32:16   *68*
Deuteronomy 32:21   *68*

2 Samuel 22:31   *8, 115*

2 Kings 17:25   *8n*

Ezra 5:12   *68*

Nehemiah 8:6   *111*

Psalm 1:2   *61*
Psalm 9:16   *107*
Psalm 17:7   *68*
Psalm 19:8   *61*
Psalm 25:6   *68*

Psalm 34:7   *61*
Psalm 78:40   *68*
Psalm 95:6   *111*
Psalm 100:1–2   *111*
Psalm 103:11   *61*
Psalm 106:32   *68*
Psalm 111:10   *61*
Psalm 116:15   *73, 163*
Psalm 134:2   *111*
Psalm 136   *24n*
Psalm 136:1–26   *149*
Psalm 149:3–4   *111*
Psalm 150:3–5   *111*

Proverbs 1:7   *61*
Proverbs 3:9-10   *109, 124*
Proverbs 6:19   *74*
Proverbs 9:8   *115, 158*
Proverbs 9:10   *61*
Proverbs 11:24   *109, 124*
Proverbs 16:3   *155*
Proverbs 16:5   *131*
Proverbs 17:9   *74*
Proverbs 19:11   *74*
Proverbs 19:17   *124*
Proverbs 21:13   *91*
Proverbs 22:4   *61*
Proverbs 23:17   *61*
Proverbs 26:12   *11*
Proverbs 28:20   *125*
Proverbs 28:23   *115*
Proverbs 28:27   *91*
Proverbs 29:23   *157*
Proverbs 30:5   *8*
Proverbs 30:6   *11, 129, 158*
Proverbs 30:8–9   *35*

Ecclesiastes 11:1-2 *124*

Isaiah 11:3 *61*
Isaiah 43:24 *147*
Isaiah 59:2 *147*
Isaiah 63:10 *147*
Isaiah 64:7 *147*
Isaiah 66:2 *61*

Jeremiah 4:4 *135n*
Jeremiah 6:6 *148*
Jeremiah 12:17 *148*
Jeremiah 15:6 *147*
Jeremiah 33:5 *147, 148*

Nahum 1:20 *68*

Zephaniah 1:12 *35*

Zechariah 1:2 *68*

Malachi 3:7–10 *108*
Malachi 3:8–9 *109*
Malachi 3:8–10 *124*

Matthew 3:2 *32*
Matthew 3:7–10 *86*
Matthew 3:8–10 *48*
Matthew 4:10 *110*
Matthew 4:17 *32*
Matthew 5:3 *131*
Matthew 5:9 *73*
Matthew 5:16 *85, 97, 100, 101, 116, 118*
Matthew 5:22 *60, 75, 128*
Matthew 5:23–26 *74*
Matthew 5:38–42 *93*
Matthew 5:43–48 *93*
Matthew 5:44 *119*
Matthew 5:46–47 *102*
Matthew 5:48 *94, 135*
Matthew 6:1–4 *101*
Matthew 6:5–13 *114*
Matthew 6:10 *34*
Matthew 6:12 *140*
Matthew 6:14–15 *140, 149*
Matthew 6:24 *125*

Matthew 7:10–28 *60*
Matthew 7:13–14 *15, 16, 36*
Matthew 7:14 *5*
Matthew 7:14–15 *x*
Matthew 7:21 *5, 23, 27, 30, 33, 43, 46, 51, 58, 120, 145*
Matthew 10:28 *59*
Matthew 10:32-33 *160*
Matthew 11:11 *128, 129, 135*
Matthew 11:20–24 *60*
Matthew 11:30 *28, 37, 117, 124, 134*
Matthew 12:31–32 *143, 149*
Matthew 12:33–37 *104, 106*
Matthew 13:22 *20, 125n*
Matthew 13:24–30 *60*
Matthew 13:40-43 *60*
Matthew 13:44 *ix*
Matthew 13:44–46 *82, 117, 150*
Matthew 13:47–50 *60*
Matthew 13:50 *6*
Matthew 15:8–9 *112, 118*
Matthew 15:14 *5, 54, 112*
Matthew 17:5 *8-9*
Matthew 18:3 *x, 5, 28, 130*
Matthew 18:4 *130*
Matthew 18:7–9 *60*
Matthew 18:14 *19*
Matthew 18:15 *74*
Matthew 18:21–22 *141*
Matthew 18:21–35 *45, 46, 82, 140, 154*
Matthew 18:34 *45n*
Matthew 18:35 *141, 147, 149*
Matthew 19:16–17 *33, 80*
Matthew 19:17 *145*
Matthew 19:18–19 *80*
Matthew 19:19 *81*
Matthew 19:22 *81*
Matthew 19:22–26 *48n, 120*
Matthew 19:23 *20*
Matthew 20:1–16 *142, 153*
Matthew 21:28–32 *48*
Matthew 21:31–32 *143*
Matthew 21:32 *49*
Matthew 21:43 *5, 16, 48, 49*
Matthew 22:1–14 *60*
Matthew 22:14 *15*
Matthew 22:21 *107*
Matthew 22:34–40 *65*
Matthew 22:36–39 *27*
Matthew 22:37–38 *81*

Matthew 22:37–40 *129*
Matthew 22:39 *66*
Matthew 23:13 *5*
Matthew 23:13–15 *54, 112*
Matthew 23:13–26 *60*
Matthew 23:23 *107*
Matthew 23:25 *37*
Matthew 23:25–26 *135*
Matthew 25:1–13 *153*
Matthew 25:14–30 *5, 98, 100, 119*
Matthew 25:30 *6*
Matthew 25:41 *6*
Matthew 25:41–46 *66, 89, 100*
Matthew 25:43 *92*
Matthew 25:45 *68, 99, 119*
Matthew 25:46 *6, 147*
Matthew 26:38 *68*
Matthew 28:18–20 *114, 115*

Mark 3:29 *143, 149*
Mark 4:19 *12*
Mark 4:24–25 *124*
Mark 8:34–38 *60*
Mark 8:36 *21*
Mark 8:38 *160*
Mark 9:7 *9*
Mark 9:42–50 *60*
Mark 9:43 *6*
Mark 9:47 *48n, 120*
Mark 10:15 *60*
Mark 10:17–19 *80*
Mark 10:17–27 *60*
Mark 10:19 *80, 81*
Mark 10:22 *81*
Mark 10:45 *31*
Mark 11:25 *60, 141, 149*
Mark 12:28–34 *60*
Mark 12:38–40 *60*
Mark 12:40 *88, 147*
Mark 12:41–44 *89*
Mark 16:16–18 *60*

Luke 1:50 *61*
Luke 3:7–14 *86, 100*
Luke 3:11 *119*
Luke 6:27 *119, 136*
Luke 6:27–31 *93, 125*
Luke 6:31 *66*
Luke 6:32–34 *101*

Luke 6:35 *102, 119*
Luke 6:37–38 *60, 142, 149*
Luke 6:38 *109, 124*
Luke 6:43–49 *60*
Luke 6:46 *30*
Luke 6:46–49 *30n, 43*
Luke 7:36–50 *154*
Luke 7:50 *42*
Luke 9:23–27 *60*
Luke 9:34–36 *9*
Luke 9:62 *60*
Luke 10:16 *60*
Luke 10:25 *64*
Luke 10:25–28 *36, 145*
Luke 10:25–37 *60, 64, 94*
Luke 10:27 *67, 119*
Luke 11:20–26 *48n, 120*
Luke 11:21–28 *60*
Luke 11:39–46 *60*
Luke 11:46 *118*
Luke 11:52 *54, 112*
Luke 12:4–5 *59*
Luke 12:4–10 *60*
Luke 12:10 *143, 149*
Luke 12:13–34 *60*
Luke 12:16–21 *125*
Luke 12:41–48 *60*
Luke 12:47 *147*
Luke 13:1–9 *60*
Luke 13:22–30 *60*
Luke 13:5 *5, 32, 46*
Luke 13:6–9 *49*
Luke 13:23–24 *47*
Luke 13:23–30 *48n, 120*
Luke 13:24 *x, 15, 28, 36, 53, 113, 119, 128, 137*
Luke 14:12–14 *60, 100, 101*
Luke 14:13–14 *91*
Luke 15:11–31 *153*
Luke 16:13–15 *60*
Luke 16:19–31 *60*
Luke 16:22–26 *7*
Luke 16:23–24 *6*
Luke 17:1–10 *60*
Luke 17:3–4 *141*
Luke 17:7–10 *99, 100, 119*
Luke 17:20–21 *48n, 120*
Luke 18:9–14 *130, 143*
Luke 18:17 *5, 130*
Luke 18:18–19 *80*

Luke 18:18–27 60
Luke 18:20 80
Luke 18:23 81
Luke 19:11–27 60
Luke 21:1–4 89
Luke 23:34 142
Luke 23:39–43 42n, 151

John 1:12–13 121
John 3:3 x, 5, 58, 120, 122
John 3:3–8 60, 61
John 3:5–8 121
John 3:16 9, 10, 29, 57, 154
John 3:36 29, 52, 60
John 4:23–24 110
John 4:24 112
John 6:40 19
John 6:49–51 29
John 6:63 137
John 8:5 43
John 8:23–24 29
John 8:24 82
John 8:31–32 145
John 8:34 31
John 8:36 31
John 8:46–47 136
John 8:47 19, 28
John 9:39 12
John 10:25–30 51n
John 12:47–50 34
John 12:49–50 9, 64n
John 12:50 145
John 14:20 68
John 14:21 64n
John 14:23 28, 64n, 68
John 14:23–24 144
John 14:24 9, 115
John 15:10–11 124
John 17:3 33
John 17:23 68, 149
John 21:15–17 64

Acts 2:38 32
Acts 3:15 31
Acts 3:19–20 32
Acts 5:32 28, 37, 136, 144
Acts 10:34 19
Acts 10:35 19
Acts 10:43 139
Acts 11:18 32

Acts 13:39 31, 139
Acts 15:1 122
Acts 16:29–31 29
Acts 17:28 68
Acts 20:34–35 97
Acts 26:18 31
Acts 26:20 34, 42, 48

Romans 1:5 35-36, 42
Romans 1:16 19
Romans 1:18 147
Romans 1:27 147
Romans 2:1 142, 149
Romans 2:5 32
Romans 2:6–7 33
Romans 2:7 146
Romans 2:8 6, 83, 100, 119, 145, 147
Romans 2:11 19
Romans 2:13 134
Romans 2:29 135
Romans 3:23 31
Romans 3:23–24 152
Romans 3:25 31, 46, 139
Romans 3:25–26 42
Romans 3:28 42
Romans 3:31 42
Romans 4:16 42
Romans 4:25 31
Romans 5:1–2 42
Romans 5:3–4 40, 159
Romans 5:9 31
Romans 5:10 31
Romans 5:17 46
Romans 5:20 46, 154
Romans 6:2–4 122
Romans 6:6 122
Romans 6:15 134
Romans 6:16 134
Romans 7:4–6 133, 134
Romans 7:7 134
Romans 8:3–4 136, 149
Romans 8:4 146
Romans 8:6 136, 137, 146
Romans 8:7 147
Romans 8:8 146
Romans 8:9–11 137
Romans 8:10 136
Romans 8:13 44, 51, 102, 145
Romans 8:14 136, 146
Romans 8:15 39

Romans 8:28 *155*
Romans 9:18 *8n*
Romans 9:30–32 *42*
Romans 10:1–4 *112*
Romans 12:1 *110*
Romans 12:2 *37, 87, 129, 131*
Romans 12:5 *67, 129*
Romans 12:9–16 *80*
Romans 12:10 *119*
Romans 12:13–16 *100*
Romans 12:17–19 *74, 93, 94*
Romans 12:17–21 *93, 100, 119*
Romans 13:1–4 *107*
Romans 13:4 *147*
Romans 13:8 *83*
Romans 13:8–10 *81*
Romans 15:1 *119*
Romans 15:1–2 *91, 100*
Romans 15:27 *95*

1 Corinthians 1:17 *7, 115*
1 Corinthians 1:20–21 *12*
1 Corinthians 3:1–4 *132*
1 Corinthians 3:18–19 *11*
1 Corinthians 6:9–10 *104, 106*
1 Corinthians 6:9–11 *31, 151*
1 Corinthians 6:13–20 *103*
1 Corinthians 6:20 *147*
1 Corinthians 9:7–12 *95*
1 Corinthians 9:14 *95*
1 Corinthians 10:12 *132*
1 Corinthians 10:13 *157*
1 Corinthians 10:24 *83, 119*
1 Corinthians 12:3 *8n*
1 Corinthians 12:10 *8n*
1 Corinthians 12:25 *67*
1 Corinthians 12:27 *67*
1 Corinthians 12:31—13:3 *70*
1 Corinthians 13:8 *78, 93*
1 Corinthians 13:8–10 *135*
1 Corinthians 14:24–25 *8n*
1 Corinthians 15:2 *ix, 16, 43*
1 Corinthians 15:58 *159*
1 Corinthians 16:14 *63*

2 Corinthians 3:7–8 *122*
2 Corinthians 3:18 *94, 121, 135*
2 Corinthians 4:7 *110*
2 Corinthians 4:18 *3, 164*
2 Corinthians 5:10 *58, 68, 147*

2 Corinthians 5:15 *84, 119*
2 Corinthians 5:17 *122*
2 Corinthians 5:17–19 *74*
2 Corinthians 5:19 *31*
2 Corinthians 7:10 *32*
2 Corinthians 9:6 *109*
2 Corinthians 9:6–8 *91*
2 Corinthians 9:6–11 *124*
2 Corinthians 9:10–11 *125n*
2 Corinthians 10:2 *35*
2 Corinthians 12:7–10 *39, 159*
2 Corinthians 13:5 *51*

Galatians 1:10 *113*
Galatians 1:11 *7*
Galatians 5:1 *31*
Galatians 5:6 *43, 81*
Galatians 5:13 *145*
Galatians 5:14 *27, 65*
Galatians 5:18 *146*
Galatians 5:19–21 *106, 155*
Galatians 5:19–25 *102, 125*
Galatians 5:21 *156, 158*
Galatians 5:22–23 *28, 38*
Galatians 5:24 *138*
Galatians 6:1 *100*
Galatians 6:1–2 *157*
Galatians 6:2 *72, 85, 87, 106, 119*
Galatians 6:6 *95, 100*
Galatians 6:8 *137, 143, 144, 146, 149*
Galatians 6:9 *100*
Galatians 6:9–10 *158*
Galatians 6:15 *122*
Galatians 6:15–16 *135*

Ephesians 2:8–9 *x, 23, 41, 42, 45, 46, 128-29*
Ephesians 2:8–10 *42*
Ephesians 2:10 *42, 128*
Ephesians 2:15–16 *31*
Ephesians 2:15–22 *67*
Ephesians 2:16 *74*
Ephesians 4:1–6 *69*
Ephesians 4:11–13 *115*
Ephesians 4:12 *117*
Ephesians 4:22–24 *122*
Ephesians 4:25 *67*
Ephesians 4:28 *97, 100*
Ephesians 4:30 *68*
Ephesians 5:1 *94*

Ephesians 5:3–7 *104*
Ephesians 5:4 *106*
Ephesians 5:6 *27, 147*
Ephesians 5:18 *158*
Ephesians 5:21 *67*
Ephesians 5:22–33 *71*
Ephesians 5:30 *67*
Ephesians 6:18 *114*

Philippians 2:3 *119*
Philippians 2:3–4 *71, 83, 100, 125*
Philippians 2:12 *48*
Philippians 2:12–13 *136*
Philippians 2:13 *123*
Philippians 2:14–15 *132*
Philippians 3:17 *145, 149*
Philippians 3:20 *113*
Philippians 4:4 *73*
Philippians 4:6–7 *114*

Colossians 1:19–20 *31, 74*
Colossians 1:21 *147*
Colossians 1:28 *116*
Colossians 2:8 *11*
Colossians 2:11 *138, 146*
Colossians 2:20–22 *117*
Colossians 2:23 *146*
Colossians 3:5 *106*
Colossians 3:5–6 *122*
Colossians 3:5–10 *104*
Colossians 3:6 *147*
Colossians 3:8 *106*
Colossians 3:9–10 *122*
Colossians 3:16 *115*
Colossians 4:2 *114*
Colossians 4:5 *97*
Colossians 6:1 *72*

1 Thessalonians 4:6 *147*
1 Thessalonians 4:11–12 *91*
1 Thessalonians 5:14 *59, 91, 99, 100, 119*

2 Thessalonians 1:8–9 *43*
2 Thessalonians 1:9 *6*
2 Thessalonians 2:13 *28, 37, 123, 136*

1 Timothy 2:6 *19*
1 Timothy 2:8 *111*
1 Timothy 4:7 *118, 137*
1 Timothy 4:16 *43*

1 Timothy 5:3–4 *88*
1 Timothy 5:8 *72, 88, 100*
1 Timothy 5:16 *88*
1 Timothy 5:17–18 *95*
1 Timothy 5:17–21 *95*
1 Timothy 5:21 *94, 100*
1 Timothy 6:10 *20, 125n*
1 Timothy 6:11–12 *106*
1 Timothy 6:17–19 *20, 125*
1 Timothy 6:18–19 *86*

2 Timothy 2:23–24 *132*
2 Timothy 3:16–17 *7, 115*
2 Timothy 4:2 *115*
2 Timothy 4:3–4 *10*

Titus 1:16 *34*
Titus 2:14 *37, 128, 134, 146*
Titus 3:5 *136*
Titus 3:10 *74*
Titus 3:10–11 *104*

Hebrews 2:2 *147*
Hebrews 3:7–11 *145*
Hebrews 3:10–11 *68*
Hebrews 3:13 *115*
Hebrews 3:18–19 *30, 30n*
Hebrews 5:8–10 *145*
Hebrews 5:9 *33*
Hebrews 6:4–6 *144*
Hebrews 6:7–10 *97*
Hebrews 6:11 *48*
Hebrews 8:9 *139*
Hebrews 8:10 *83, 139*
Hebrews 8:12 *139*
Hebrews 9:1 *111*
Hebrews 10:24 *49, 115*
Hebrews 10:26 *52, 53, 145*
Hebrews 10:26–31 *44, 47, 59, 144, 145, 146, 147, 148, 149*
Hebrews 10:27 *6*
Hebrews 10:30 *74, 94*
Hebrews 10:35–39 *157*
Hebrews 10:36–39 *30, 30n*
Hebrews 10:38 *35*
Hebrews 12:7–8 *40*
Hebrews 12:10–11 *40, 107, 159*
Hebrews 12:14–15 *73*
Hebrews 12:28–29 *111*
Hebrews 13:1 *119*

Hebrews 13:2   *100*
Hebrews 13:1–3   *91*
Hebrews 13:2–3   *119*
Hebrews 13:5   *159*
Hebrews 13:16   *83*
Hebrews 13:17   *106*

James 1:2–4   *40*
James 1:15   *145*
James 1:18   *121*
James 1:26   *74, 104*
James 1:27   *91, 100, 119, 131*
James 2:1–4   *95*
James 2:5   *20*
James 2:8   *81*
James 2:8–9   *94, 95, 100*
James 2:12–13   *141, 149*
James 2:24   *35*
James 2:26   *5, 23, 35, 42*
James 3:9–10   *67, 104*
James 3:18   *73*
James 3:24   *23*
James 4:4   *132*
James 4:5   *68*
James 4:12   *10, 61*
James 4:14   *116*
James 4:17   *95, 96, 100, 119*
James 5:5   *37*
James 5:19–20   *107, 148, 149*
James 5:20   *157*

1 Peter 1:2   *28, 37, 123, 136*
1 Peter 1:14   *132, 145*
1 Peter 1:17   *23, 42, 48, 58, 132*
1 Peter 1:22–23   *121*
1 Peter 1:25   *8, 115*
1 Peter 2:2   *131*
1 Peter 2:13–17   *106*
1 Peter 2:24   *31*
1 Peter 3:1–7   *70, 71*
1 Peter 3:21   *146*
1 Peter 4:8   *70, 148, 149*
1 Peter 4:11   *94*
1 Peter 5:2   *134*

2 Peter 1:5–7   *47, 128, 128n*
2 Peter 1:10–11   *16. 43, 47*
2 Peter 1:20–21   *7, 115*

2 Peter 2:4   *6*
2 Peter 2:4–10   *60, 146*
2 Peter 2:9   *147*
2 Peter 2:9–10   *107*
2 Peter 2:20   *94*
2 Peter 2:20–22   *144, 149*
2 Peter 3:9   *5, 19, 32, 46*
2 Peter 3:13–14   *36*
2 Peter 3:16   *44, 113*
2 Peter 3:17   *43*

1 John 1:8   *139, 145*
1 John 1:9   *140, 145, 146, 149*
1 John 1:10   *146, 149*
1 John 2:1–2   *145*
1 John 2:2   *19*
1 John 2:3–4   *27, 34*
1 John 2:15–17   *125*
1 John 2:17   *33, 147*
1 John 2:29   *121*
1 John 3:6   *145*
1 John 3:9   *103, 144, 145*
1 John 3:15   *67*
1 John 3:16–18   *82*
1 John 3:17   *119*
1 John 3:17–18   *100*
1 John 3:18   *27, 43, 69*
1 John 3:23   *81*
1 John 3:24   *28, 144*
1 John 4:12   *28, 144*
1 John 4:15   *144*
1 John 4:16   *59*
1 John 4:20–21   *65*
1 John 4:21   *67*
1 John 5:1   *144*
1 John 5:2   *147*
1 John 5:3   *27, 64*
1 John 5:3–4   *37, 117, 120, 125, 132*
1 John 5:17   *139*

Jude 1:7   *6, 103, 106, 148*
Jude 10   *36*

Revelation 3:15–17   *34*
Revelation 19:2   *104*
Revelation 21:8   *103, 106*
Revelation 21:27   *103, 106*
Revelation 22:12   *58, 68*

About the Author

TIMOTHY W. BURROW, son of a Cumberland Presbyterian preacher, has one son, John-Michael, who attends the University of Tennessee, Knoxville. Mr. Burrow currently practices law with Burrow & Cravens, P.C., in Nashville as a construction and real estate lawyer and construction arbitrator; he also provides expert witness services on construction cases.

He graduated from the University of Tennessee, Knoxville, with a Bachelor of Architecture degree, and thereafter practiced as an architect for 14 years and a licensed contractor for two years before graduating from the Nashville School of Law in the top ten percent of his class and becoming a lawyer in 1995.

Mr. Burrow is a board member with The Jefferson Society, whose members comprise those with dual degrees in architecture and law. He is also a member of the American Institute of Architects, Nashville Bar Association, Tennessee Bar Association, American Bar Association, as well as various construction related associations.

Mr. Burrow's passions are in resolving disputes, analyzing Scripture, and, of course, discussing what it takes to get to heaven. For fun he finds pleasure in just about any outdoor activity.